DATE DUE

APR 0 1 02			

DEMCO 38-297

The Cultural Shaping
of Accounting

THE CULTURAL SHAPING
OF ACCOUNTING

Ahmed Riahi-Belkaoui

QUORUM BOOKS
Westport, Connecticut • London

Library of Congress Cataloging-in-Publication Data

Riahi-Belkaoui, Ahmed.
    The cultural shaping of accounting / Ahmed Riahi-Belkaoui.
      p. cm.
    Includes bibliographical references and index.
    ISBN 0–89930–953–4
    1. Accounting—Social aspects. 2. Comparative accounting.
    3. Cultural relativism.   I. Title.
    HF5657.R49 1995
    657—dc20   94–45274

British Library Cataloguing in Publication Data is available.

Library of Congress Catalog Card Number: 94–45274
ISBN: 0–89930–953–4

First published in 1995

Quorum Books, 88 Post Road West, Westport, CT 06881
An imprint of Greenwood Publishing Group, Inc.

Printed in the United States of America

The paper used in this book complies with the
Permanent Paper Standard issued by the National
Information Standards Organization (Z39.48–1984).

10 9 8 7 6 5 4 3 2 1

Copyright Acknowledgments

The author and publisher are grateful for permission to reprint the following copyrighted material:

Ajay Adhikari and Rasoul H. Tondkar, "Environmental Factors Influencing Accounting Disclosure Requirements of Global Stock Exchanges," *Journal of International Financial Management and Accounting* 4 (1992): 102–4.

Ahmed Belkaoui, "Accounting and Language," *Journal of Accounting Literature* 8 (1989): 281–92.

J.R. Cohen et al., "Culture-Based Ethical Conflicts Confronting Multinational Accounting Firms," *Accounting Horizons* (September 1993): 1–13.

G.L. Harrison and J.L. McKinnon, "Culture and Accounting Change: A New Perspective on Corporate Reporting Regulations and Accounting Policy Formulation," *Accounting, Organizations and Society* 11, no. 3 (1986): 233–52.

E.L. Pavlik et al., "Executive Compensation: Issues and Research," *Journal of Accounting Literature* 12 (1993): 143–53.

Ahmed Riahi-Belkaoui, "Cultural Determinism and Compensation Practices," *International Journal of Commerce and Management* 4, no. 3 (1994): 76–83.

Ahmed Riahi-Belkaoui and R.D. Picur, "Cultural Determinism and the Perception of Accounting Concepts," *The International Journal of Accounting* 26 (1991): 118–30.

To my family, here and there.

Contents

Exhibits   xi

Preface   xiii

1. Cultural Relativism in Accounting   1
   Appendix 1.1. Accounting and Language   27

2. Cultural Determinism and the Perception
   of Accounting Concepts   39
   Appendix 2.1. Questionnaire   67
   Appendix 2.2. Culture-Based Ethical Conflicts Confronting
   *   Multinational Accounting Firms*   71

3. Cultural Determinism and Professional Self-Regulation   85
   Appendix 3.1. Culture and Accounting Change: A New
   *   Perspective on Corporate Reporting Regulation and*
   *   Accounting Policy Formulation*   99

4. Cultural Determinism and Accounting Disclosure
   Requirements of Global Stock Exchanges   119
   Appendix 4.1. Disclosure Scoring Sheet   128

5. Cultural Determinism and Compensation Practices   133

   Index   155

Exhibits

1.1. Cultural Relativism in Accounting   4

2.1. Accounting Concepts' Salience in
Three-Dimensional Space   58

2.2. Results of the Analysis of Variance on Three Dimensions'
Salience   59

2.3. Regression Results on the Dimensions' Salience   59

3.1. Countries and Professional Self-Regulation Score   95

3.2. Regression Results   96

4.1. Countries and Data   123

4.2. Results of Cross-Sectional Regressions (n=32)   125

5.1. Compensation and Performance   134

5.2. List of Countries Used   147

5.3. Pay for Time Worked in U.S. Dollars   147

5.4. Hourly Direct Pay in U.S. Dollars   148

5.5. Hourly Compensation Costs in U.S. Dollars   149

Preface

All of our activities are touched by culture. Accounting is not immune to this law. Culture may be viewed as accounting's medium. Culture affects all facets of the accounting environment. This book shows that culture:

1. determines the judgement/decision process in accounting (Chapter 1);
2. explains the intercultural differences in the perception of accounting concepts (Chapter 2);
3. explains the differences in the degree of professional self-regulation in accounting internationally (Chapter 3);
4. explains the differences in the levels of disclosure requirements of stock exchanges internationally (Chapter 4); and
5. is an important determinant of compensation practices internationally (Chapter 5).

The book should be of value to all those interested in international accounting issues, including professional accountants, business executives, teachers and researchers, and students.

Many people have helped in the development of this book. I received considerable assistance from the University of Illinois at Chicago research assistants, specially Claire Howard. I also thank Eric Valentine, John Donohue, and the entire production team at Quorum Books for their continuous and intelligent support. Finally, to Janice and Hédi, thanks for making everything possible and enjoyable.

—

The Cultural Shaping
of Accounting

Cultural Relativism
in Accounting

INTRODUCTION

This chapter examines the concept of cultural relativism in accounting. This concept postulates that culture shapes the cognitive functioning of individuals faced with an accounting and auditing phenomenon. Before presentation of the model, the chapter elaborates on the different notions of culture.

NOTIONS OF CULTURE

The concept of culture has been subjected to various interpretations. In fact, some anthropologists have stated that culture in the abstract can be explained only by reference to specific cultures.[1] Anthropologists approach culture in at least three different ways: (1) the cultural universals approach, (2) the value systems approach, and (3) the systems approach.[2]

The cultural universals approach focuses on identifying certain universals common to all cultures, which does allow an examination of cultures in terms of how they contribute to these variables. An example of such a list is provided by G.P. Murdock.[3]

The value systems approach focuses on classifying cultures according to value systems. Instruments used to assess values among cultures include the Allport, Vernon, and Lindzey instrument,[4] Morris's "way of life" instrument,[5] Kluckhohn and Strodtbeck's value theory,[6] Sarnoff's human value index,[7] and Rokeach's value survey.[8]

The systems approach focuses on the systems that make up a given culture. P.R. Harris and R.T. Moran identified eight subsystems in a culture: kinship, education, economy, politics, religion, association, health, and recreation.[9]

Some anthropologists view culture as information doubly coded—once chemically in the brain as memory, and once externally as a language, behavior, material, or document, and as a cultural pool from which each individual, each dyad, each group draws its particular culture.[10]

In short, culture remains the basis of anthropological research. Anthropologists differ as to what the concept of culture means, although they generally agree that it is learned rather than logically transmitted, that it is shared by the members of a group, and that it is the foundation of the human way of life.[11] There is also a consensus on the issue of cultural utility in the sense that cultural practices have "functions" or reflect a society's "adaptations" to its environment.

[C]ulture is man's primary mode of achieving reproductive success. Hence particular sociocultural systems are arrangements of patterned behavior, thought, and feeling that contribute to the survival and reproduction of particular social groups. Traits contributing to the maintenance of a system may be said to have a *positive function* with respect to that system. Viable systems may be regarded as consisting largely of positive-functioned traits, since the contrary assumption would lead us to expect the system's extinction.[12]

[C]ustoms which diminish the survival chances of a society are not likely to persist. . . . Those customs of a society that enhance survival chances are *adaptive* and are likely to persist. Hence we assume that, if a society has survived to be described in the annals of anthropology, much if not most of its cultural repertoires is adaptive, or was at one time.[13]

That cultural customs can be explained in practical materialist terms is well explained by anthropologist Marvin Harris in his popular *Cows, Pigs, Wars and Witches: The Riddle of Culture.*[14]

Various concepts of culture exist in anthropology suggesting different themes for accounting research.[15]

1. Following Malinowski's functionalism,[16] culture may be viewed as an instrument serving biological and psychological needs. Applying this definition to accounting research suggests the perception of accounting in each culture as a specific social instrument for task accomplishment and the analysis of cross-cultural or comparative accounting.

2. Following Radcliffe-Brown's structural functionalism,[17] culture may be viewed as an adaptive regulatory mechanism that unites individuals with social structures. Applying this definition to accounting research suggests the perception

of accounting in each culture as an adaptive instrument existing by process of exchange with the environment and the analysis of an accounting culture.

3. Following Goodenough's ethnoscience,[18] culture may be viewed as a system of shared cognitions. The human mind thus generates culture by means of a finite number of rules. Applying this definition to accounting suggests that accounting may be viewed as a system of knowledge that members of each culture share to varying degrees and the analysis of accounting as cognition.

4. Following Geertz's symbolic anthropology,[19] culture may be viewed as a system of shared symbols and meanings. Applying this definition to accounting research suggests that accounting may be viewed as a pattern of symbolic discourse or language and the analysis of accounting as language.

5. Following Levi-Strauss's structuralism,[20] culture may be viewed as a projection of the mind's universal unconscious infrastructure. Applying this definition to accounting suggests that accounting may be viewed in each culture as the manifestation of unconscious processes and the analysis of unconscious processes in accounting.

CULTURAL RELATIVISM IN ACCOUNTING

The Cultural Relativism Model

Edward T. Hall has stated that

culture is man's medium; there is not one aspect of human life that is not touched and altered by culture. This means personalities, how people express themselves (including show of emotions), the way they think, how they move, how problems are solved, how their cities are planned and laid out, how transportation systems function and are organized, as well as how economic and government systems are put together and function.[21]

This point applies well to accounting, where culture can be viewed as accounting's medium. Culture in essence determines the judgment/decision process in accounting. The model, as illustrated in Exhibit 1.1, postulates that culture, through its components, elements, and dimensions, dictates the organizational structures adopted, the micro-organizational behavior, and the cognitive functioning of individuals, in such a way as to ultimately affect their judgment/decision process when they are faced with an accounting and/or auditing phenomenon.

Operationalization of Culture

This model avoids the two main problems that had beset earlier operationalization and use of culture: the equating of culture with nations and the ad hoc use of culture as a residual factor in explaining the variations that had not been explained by other factors.[22] Culture is viewed as col-

Exhibit 1.1
Cultural Relativism in Accounting

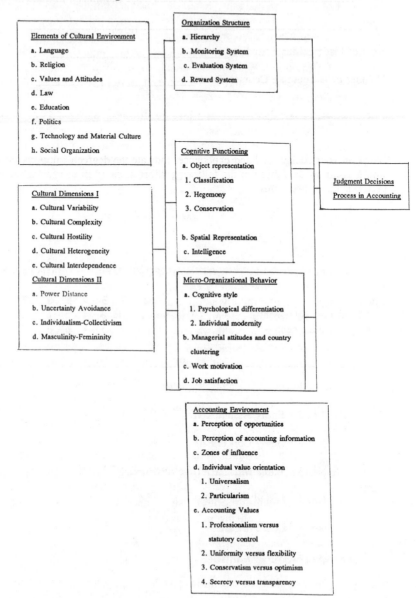

Culture

Elements of Cultural Environment
a. Language
b. Religion
c. Values and Attitudes
d. Law
e. Education
f. Politics
g. Technology and Material Culture
h. Social Organization

Cultural Dimensions I
a. Cultural Variability
b. Cultural Complexity
c. Cultural Hostility
d. Cultural Heterogeneity
e. Cultural Interdependence
Cultural Dimensions II
a. Power Distance
b. Uncertainty Avoidance
c. Individualism-Collectivism
d. Masculinity-Femininity

Organization Structure
a. Hierarchy
b. Monitoring System
c. Evaluation System
d. Reward System

Cognitive Functioning
a. Object representation
1. Classification
2. Hegemony
3. Conservation

b. Spatial Representation
c. Intelligence

Micro-Organizational Behavior
a. Cognitive style
1. Psychological differentiation
2. Individual modernity
b. Managerial attitudes and country
clustering
c. Work motivation
d. Job satisfaction

Accounting Environment
a. Perception of opportunities
b. Perception of accounting information
c. Zones of influence
d. Individual value orientation
1. Universalism
2. Particularism
e. Accounting Values
1. Professionalism versus
statutory control
2. Uniformity versus flexibility
3. Conservatism versus optimism
4. Secrecy versus transparency

Judgment Decisions
Process in Accounting

lective mental programming[23]—that is, an ideological system forming the backdrop for human activity and providing people with a theory of reality.[24] This backdrop is composed of distinct elements and includes definite dimensions.

Some cultural elements generally are assumed to affect the conduct of international business. Each of these elements—language, religion, values and attitudes, law, education, politics, technology and material culture, and social organization—is assumed in this cultural relativism model to have the potential of dictating the organizational structures adopted, the cognitive functioning of individuals, and micro-organizational behavior, that may shape the judgment/decision process in accounting.

Cultures vary along five dimensions: cultural variability, cultural complexity, cultural hostility, cultural heterogeneity, and cultural interdependence.[25] The first three dimensions refer to conditions within cultures, while the latter two refer to conditions among cultures. These dimensions may be seen as potential sources of problems for the multinational corporation:

1. *Cultural variability* generates uncertainty, which calls for organizational flexibility and adaptability;

2. *Cultural complexity* raises the difficulty of understanding, which necessitates organizational and individual contexting and preparation;

3. *Cultural hostility* threatens goal attainment and survival, which demands the maintenance of social acceptability;

4. *Cultural heterogeneity* hinders centralized decision making with information overload, which calls for decentralization; and

5. *Cultural independence* increases the vulnerability of an organization to intergroup conflict, which necessitates less autonomy for individual subsidiaries and more system-wide coordination.[26]

This cultural relativism model assumes that differences in these five dimensions generate different cultural environments that have the potential of dictating the organizational structures adopted, the cognitive functioning of individuals, and the micro-organizational behavior that may shape the judgment/decision process in accounting.

Cultures also vary along four dimensions that reflect the cultural orientations of a country and explain 50 percent of the differences in value systems among countries:[27] (1) individualism versus collectivism, (2) large versus small power distance, (3) strong versus weak uncertainty avoidance, and (4) masculinity versus femininity.

Individualism versus collectivism is a dimension that represents the degree of integration a society maintains among its members or the relationship between an individual and his/her fellow individuals. While

individualists are expected to take care of themselves and their immediate families only, collectivists are expected to remain emotionally integrated into in-groups, which protect them in exchange for unquestioning
loyalty.

Large versus small power distance represents the extent to which members of a society accept the unequal distribution of power in institutions
and organizations. In large power distance societies there is a tendency
for people to accept a hierarchical order in which everyone has a place
which needs no justification, whereas in small power distance societies
people tend to live for equality and demand justification for any existing
power inequalities.

Strong versus weak uncertainty avoidance is a dimension that represents
the degree to which the members of a society feel uncomfortable with
uncertainty and ambiguity. In strong uncertainty avoidance societies people are intolerant of ambiguity and try to control it at all costs, whereas
in weak uncertainty avoidance societies people are more tolerant of ambiguity and tend to live with it.

Masculinity versus femininity is a dimension that represents the nature
of the social division of sex roles. Masculine roles imply a preference for
achievement, assertiveness, making money, sympathy for the strong, and
the like. Feminine roles imply a preference for warm relationships, modesty, care for the weak, preservation of the environment, concern for the
quality of life, and so on.

This cultural relativism model assumes that differences among these
four dimensions create different cultural arenas that have the potential of
dictating the organizational structures adopted, the type of cognitive functioning, and the microorganizational behavior that may shape the judg-
ment/decision process in accounting.

Culture and Organizational Structure

The cultural relativism model assumes that culture, through its elements
and dimensions, dictates the type of organizational structure. The idea was
first advanced by J. Child, who stated that culture affects the design of
organizational structure,[28] strongly refuting the "culture-free" contingency
theory of organizational structure proposed by D.J. Hickson and colleagues.[29-31] In fact, A. Sorge argued that all facts that bear upon organizational practices do so in the form of cultural constructs, and that
organizations develop through a "nonrational" process of experimentation
that is wholly cultured.[32]

There is no culture-free context of organization, because even if organizational
solutions or contexts are similar, they are always culturally constructed and very
imperfectly interpreted as the reaction to a given constraint. Culture enters or-

ganization through artful, unselfconscious, piecemeal experimentations with alternatives in business policy, finance, work/organization, industrial relations, education and training, and many other factors.[33]

Uma Sekaran and Carol R. Snodgrass carry the argument one step further by offering ideas on how specific cultural dimensions affect particular structural elements.[34] More specifically, they attempt to match the four structural aspects of the organization—hierarchy, monitoring system, evaluation system, and reward system—with the four cultural dimensions identified by Hofstede to synchronize with the preferred modes of behavior of organizational members.

Hierarchies refer to how organizations distribute power among their members, while power distance refers to how a society accepts the fact that power in institutions and organizations is unequally distributed. It follows that the situation for large power distance culture groups calls for centralized and rigid hierarchies followed by emergent behavior of dependence and counterdependence, while the situation for low power distance cultural groups calls for decentralized and fluid hierarchies followed by a behavior of independence.

The monitoring system refers to the process of collection and dissemination of information on performance, while uncertainty avoidance refers to the certainty of an unknown future and the difference in the way people react to it by experiencing different levels of anxiety. It follows that the situation for weak uncertainty avoidance calls for a simplistic monitoring system, while the situation for high uncertainty avoidance calls for a complete and comprehensive monitoring system followed by low levels of anxiety.

The evaluation system refers to the process of appraising the effectiveness and efficiency of organizational individual performance. Individual-collectivism refers to the type of relationship between a group and one of its members. It follows that a situation for individualistic cultural groups calls for an evaluation system based on individual achievement followed by a calculative behavior, while a situation for collectivistic cultural groups calls for an evaluation system based on organizational performance followed by a moralistic behavior.

The reward system refers to the process of bestowing rewards for organizational or individual performance, while masculinity-femininity refers to the nature of the social division of sex roles. It follows that a situation for "masculine" cultural groups calls for a reward system based on money, power, individual recognition and promotion, challenging assignments, status symbols, and the like, and catering to their machismo ideals, while a situation for "feminine" cultural groups calls for a reward system based on good quality of work life, security, a sense of belonging, a cooperative work system, and catering to their androgynous ideals.

Micro-Organizational Behavior and Culture

Cross-cultural research on micro-organizational behavior has examined various issues including cognitive style, worker motivation, job satisfaction, and other important managerial attitudes and behavior, and has highlighted the differences across various cultures.[35]

Research on cognitive style focuses on cultural differences in the structural aspects of an individual's cognitive system. It relied on the concept of psychological differentiation introduced by Witken, Dyk, Faterson, Goodenough, and Karp,[36] and used by Witkin and Berry[37] for an understanding of the effects of subjective culture on individual behavior. Known as the theory of psychological differentiation, it relies on field dependence and field-independence measures to categorize people along the dimension of field of articulation. Cultural differences were found in the level of field articulation among cultural groups in several countries.[38] Besides the concept of field dependence, the cognitive style approach known as individual modernity was used in cross-cultural research to explain how cultures change from traditional to modern.[39]

Research on attitudes and values focuses on cultural differences rather than similarities in personal, work-related, and ancestral values and attitudes. Various studies focus on a clustering of countries in terms of managerial and worker attitudes and values. Simcha Ronen and Oded Shenkar present a review of the published literature on country clustering and propose a map that integrates and synthesizes the available data.[40] The variables examined in these clustering studies include work goal importance, need deficiency, fulfillment and job satisfaction, managerial and organizational variables, and work role and interpersonal orientation. The resulting clusters discriminate on the basis of language, religion, and geography. Well-defined clusters are the Anglo, Germanic, Nordic, Latin-European, and Latin American ones. Ill-defined clusters are those describing the Far East and Arab countries, as well as countries described as independent (i.e., Israel and Japan). Areas in Africa have not been studied at all, while those in the Middle East and Far East have not been studied sufficiently. The review is, however, criticized by Peter Blunt[41] for alleged ethnocentrism and technocentrism, defined as a lack of interdisciplinary approach in organizational studies.

Research on work motivation examines cross-cultural differences in motivation using one of the following theoretical bases: Atkinson's expectancy theory,[42] McClelland's achievement motivational theory,[43] vocation- and achievement-related motivation,[44] and Adam's equity theory.[45]

Research on job satisfaction focuses on cross-cultural differences in the relationships between satisfaction and other variables of interest, such as absenteeism or productivity. These studies rely on the following theoretical bases: Maslow's need theory,[46] the importance of various job dimensions,[47] frame reference theory,[48] environmental theory,[49] Herzberg's two-factor theory,[50] and the alienation hypothesis.[51]

Culture and Accounting Environment Variables

Culture is an important variable affecting a country's accounting environment. It has also been argued that accounting is in fact determined by the culture of a given country,[52] and that lack of consensus among different countries on what constitutes proper accounting methods results because the purpose of accounting is cultural, not technical.[53] Various approaches examining the impact of culture on the accounting environment have been taken.

J. Acheson found that while a native system does not permanently block responsiveness to existing opportunities, it confuses the view of opportunities, leading to many poor decisions, and hence plays a critical role in influencing further business decisions.[54]

G. Chevalier examined the perception of accounting information by French- and English-speaking Canadians.[55] Perceptions did not differ with regard to the importance of conventional published financial information, which had been expected to differ for the French Canadians, who place more importance on additional and nonconventional information such as data on human resources, earnings forecasts, and management philosophy. Chevalier's subjects were essentially students from the English and Anglophone sections of Canada. Other studies have investigated investors and financial analysts from various cultural settings. L.S. Chang and K.S. Most investigated the use of financial statements by individual investors, institutional investors, and financial analysts from the United States, Great Britain, and New Zealand—all of which have large capital markets and well-organized stock exchanges which tend to function in a similar manner.[56] The results showed a strong belief in the importance of corporate annual reports as a source of information for investment decisions and an even stronger belief that the most important parts of the corporate annual report for this purpose were those pertaining to the financial data. The study also examined the composition of the three financial user groups and found institutional investors and financial analysts to be largely alike, while individual investors were more diverse.

Because the decisions of most investors in any country are greatly influenced by the opinions of financial analysts, A. Belkaoui, A. Kahl, and J. Peyrard examined the needs of financial analysts in Canada, the United States, and Europe.[57] Any differences in perception were hypothesized to be primarily due to the differences in the European and U.S. methods of investing. The European approach has been typically more debt-oriented, with analysis concentrated on the balance sheet. In brief, the method requires the preparation of three reports: profit and loss account, financing table, and balance sheet. Reports are then presented in vertical form, high-lighting a set of totals and subtotals deemed to be of interest to financial analysts. These reports offer a convenient means of achieving comparisons of European accounting information. In contrast, the U.S. method is oriented more toward equity investment, the income statement, and corporate earning power. As expected, the study demonstrates that there is a high degree of consensus on the part of North American financial analysts on information of value to equity investors, but there is quite a divergence of opinion when Americans are compared with their European counterparts. This divergence has been attributed to institutional differences in the accounting and investment environments of Europe and North America, as well as to differences in outlook, with Europeans more interested in balance sheet information, while North Americans tend to be more concerned about the income statement.

While not necessarily restricted to accounting, various studies have attempted to identify the determinants of differences in accounting systems that have resulted in "zones of influence." One type of study attempted to identify relevant environmental factors, including culture, and link them to national accounting practices.[58-65] The second type of study attempted to explain empirically the patterns discovered by reference to empirical factors.[66-74]

The impact of the cultural environment and individual value orientation on financial disclosure has been examined by B.L. Jaggi.[75] He argues that culture has an impact on the value orientation of managers, resulting in different disclosure decisions. Jaggi relies on concepts developed by Talcott Parsons and Edward A. Shils[76] that allow the identification of the different patterns of value orientations of individuals in different cultures, namely "universalism," to represent a value orientation toward institutionalized obligation to society and "particularism," representing a value orientation toward institutional obligations to friendship. Universalism calls for commitment to disclosure of relatively reliable information, while particularism calls for relatively low reliability of information disclosed. Jaggi suggests two hypotheses:

> Hypothesis 1: The reliability is likely to differ with differences in the value orientations of managers from different countries. Accounting principles and procedures will vary to respond to the needs of individual countries, and to ensure reliability in a given set of cultural environments.
>
> Hypothesis 2: As a result of the prevailing cultural environment in the developing countries, the reliability of financial disclosure is not expected to be high unless disclosure standards are set.[77]

Without empirically testing these two important hypotheses, Jaggi goes on to suggest that the procedures for developing accounting principles should be modified to suit the cultural environment.

The impact of culture on accounting values and on accounting systems has been examined by S.J. Gray.[78] Using Hofstede's classification of cultural dimensions, Gray presents a model that links the value systems of accountants to societal values with special reference to work-related values, and in turn the accounting values' impact on accounting systems. The accounting values derived from the accounting literature include the following:

Professionalism versus statutory control—A preference for the exercise of individual professional judgment and the maintenance of professional self-regulation as opposed to compliance with prescriptive legal requirements and statutory control.

Uniformity versus flexibility—A preference for the enforcement of uniform accounting practices between companies and for the consistent use of such practices over time as opposed to flexibility in accordance with the perceived circumstances of individual companies.

Conservatism versus optimism—A preference for a cautious approach to measurement to cope with the uncertainty of future events as opposed to a more transparent, open, and publicly accountable approach.

Secrecy versus transparency—A preference for confidentiality and the restriction of disclosure information about the business only to those who are closely involved with its management and financing as opposed to a more transparent, open, and publicly accountable approach.[79]

The model demonstrates that professionalism is positively related to individualism and negatively related to uncertainty avoidance and poser distance; uniformity is positively related to uncertainty avoidance and negatively related to individualism; conservatism is positively related to uncertainty avoidance and negatively related to individualism and masculinity; and secrecy is positively related to uncertainty avoidance and power distance and negatively related to individualism and masculinity.

Cognitive Functioning

How people learn and think represents the study of human cognition. Cultural differences in cognitive functioning have also been subject to debate. Do people from different cultures perform differently on tasks that require certain cognitive skills? Two general hypotheses have been proposed. One maintains that cognitive processes are similar in individuals in different cultures, the other that cognitive processes are subject to cultural differences.[80,81] Evidence has been presented in support of both positions.[82,83] A third "situationist" hypothesis argues that cultural differences depend on the particular situation in the sense that "cultural differences in cognition reside more in the situations in which particular cognitive processes are applied than in the existence of a process in one cultural group and its absence in another."[84]

The debate needs to be continued in accounting research to determine whether people from different cultures will perform differently on tasks that require certain cognitive skills. Certain conditions need to be met in order to be able to usefully interpret potential cultural differences in cognitive functioning in an accounting context.

When we consider intellectual growth or style in different cultures, we are confronted by three requirements. We need to obtain . . . some picture of skills common to people from many backgrounds, as well as skills that differentiate among them. At the same time, we need to find the features of milieu that may account for the similarities and differences in skills. And finally, . . . we have to ask as we transpose a task from one culture to another, whether the same answer means the same thing in both worlds.[85]

To meet these requirements, two conditions need to be met. One is to assure the absence of ambiguous communication between the participants of the experiment and the preparers of the tasks, as differences in the way people perform may reflect different understandings of the requirements rather than differences in cognitive functioning. The second is to ensure that the participants are truly representative of their respective cultures.

Are there any differences in the cognitive strategies used by people from different cultures when they represent information about objects? To answer this question, various studies have examined potential differences in classification, memory, and conservation.

There may be cultural differences in the way people classify objects, through the use of different attributes. Cultural differences in classification tasks have been observed, although the variation may be attributable in some cases to differences in education and differences in familiarity with the items to be classified.[86] Similarly cultural differences in ability to abstract or to think in generalities have been observed in sorting tasks. However, in constrained classification tasks where the subjects learn to identify objects consistently on the basis of some feature, the skill in performing the task increases with age[87] and with education level.[88]

The recall of information from memory and its relation to culture is another research question of interest to object representation. In most experiments assessing the potential for cultural differences in the recall of information, age and education level were better related to the ways people from different cultures assess their memories.[89-91]

The concept of conservation, as introduced in Piaget's theory, refers to the ability of people to recognize the identity of objects or substances in spite of changes in their appearance. Cultural differences in the performance of conservation tasks are another research question of interest to object representation. While there are some obvious common problems due to differences in testing and scoring methods (age range of subjects, amount and kind of verbalization elicited from subjects, and language of testing), the results of experiments confirm the existence of a similar sequence of conservation across cultures and the existence of a "lag" in development of conservation among some cultures.[92-94] Education, although not necessarily formal, as well as familiarity with the task are also associated with differences in conservation performance.

Are there any differences in the cognitive strategies used by people from different cultures when they organize and use spatial information? Various studies have examined the potential for cultural difference in spatial reference systems. Different spatial reference systems were found to be used by Puluwat sailors navigating among the islands in the Western Pacific,[95] and by the Temme in West Africa.[96] Other studies determined that cultural differences in the degree of field dependence are a result of differences in child rearing and other socialization practices.[97] The evidence tends toward the existence of cultural differences in the organization and use of spatial information. More evidence is needed, however, to ensure that the participants are more representative of their culture and are more familiar with tasks they can relate to.

There are also potential cultural differences in competence in cognitive behavior, which is equivalent to the Western notion of intelligence. A good definition follows:

Intelligence, a concept within the area of individual differences, reduces itself to two essentials, the power of the mind, and the skills through which this power expresses itself. The former aspect comes nearest to what the man in the street means by intelligence. It can be defined as "the ability to learn," "the capacity for understanding," "the ability to perceive essential relations between things," "insight into the nature of things." The "machines" through which this power expresses itself provide the foundation of abilities—from the highest abilities such as the solving of mathematical equations, right down to the simplest such as tying one's bootlaces.[98]

Attempts to provide possible cultural bases for differences in general intelligence have been criticized for a number of reasons:

1. most tests of intelligence are culture-specific;
2. conceptual abilities are used as the skills to be assessed as intelligence, while members of non-European cultures are known to think concretely;[99]
3. the environmental conditions between different cultural groups are not necessarily identical;[100]
4. contact with Western culture, familiarity with test materials, and conditions of testing affect the results;[101-103]

5. rural versus urban environment, education level, and early nutrition can also affect general intellectual development, a phenomenon known as the deficit hypothesis.[104]

Berry, however, emphasizes that one must accept that it is clever to do different things in different cultural systems, and if inferences about intelligence are made, the original observations must be based upon an adequate sample of what people are able to do in their own cultural system.[105] A similar point is made by Vernon:

We must try to discard the idea that intelligence (i.e. intelligence b) is a kind of universal faculty, a trait which is the same (apart from variations in amount) in all cultural groups. Clearly, it develops differently in different physical and cultural environments. It should be regarded as a name for all the various cognitive skills which are developed in, and valued by, the group. In Western civilization it refers mainly to grasping relations and symbolic thinking, and this permeates to some extent all the abilities we show at school, at work, or in daily life. We naturally tend to evaluate the intelligence of other ethnic groups on the same criteria, though it would surely be more psychologically sound to recognize that such groups require, and stimulate, the growth of different mental as well as physical skills for coping with their particular environments, i.e., that they possess different intelligences.[106]

CONCLUSIONS

The essence of cultural relativism in accounting is the presence of a cultural process that is assumed to guide the judgment/decision process in accounting. The model in this chapter postulates that culture, through its components, elements, and dimensions, dictates the organizational structures adopted, micro-organizational behavior, the accounting environment, and the cognitive functioning of individuals faced with an accounting and/or auditing phenomenon.

It is important to also realize the following points:

1. Cultural relativism affects not only accounting performance, as is argued in this chapter, but also economic performance.
2. Cultural relativism is different from religious relativism whereby religion affects accounting performance.
3. Cultural relativism is different from linguistic relativism whereby language affects accounting performance, as is argued in Appendix 1.1.

NOTES

1. Leslie White, *The Science of Culture* (New York: Grove Press, 1949).
2. Simcha Ronen, *Comparative and Multinational Management* (New York: Wiley, 1986), pp. 20–27.

3. G.P. Murdock, "Common Denominator of Cultures," in R. Linten, ed., *The Science of Man in the World Crises* (New York: Columbia University Press, 1945), pp. 12–42.

4. G.W. Allport, P.E. Vernon, and Q. Lindzey, *A Study of Values* (Boston: Houghton Mifflin, 1960).

5. C. Morris, *Varieties of Human Value* (Chicago: University of Chicago Press, 1956).

6. F.R. Kluckhohn and F. Strodtbeck, *Variations in Value Orientations* (Westport, Conn.: Greenwood Press, 1973).

7. I. Sarnoff, *Society with Tears* (Secaucus, N.J.: Citadel Press, 1966).

8. J. Rokeach, *The Nature of Human Values* (New York: Free Press, 1966).

9. P.R. Harris and R.T. Moran, *Managing Cultural Differences* (Houston: Cruff, 1979).

10. Paul Bohannan, "Rethinking Culture: A Project for Current Anthropologists," *Current Anthropology* 14, no. 4 (October 1973): 357–65.

11. Harris and Moran, *Managing Cultural Differences*, p. 8.

12. Marvin Harris, *Culture, Man and Nature* (New York: Thomas Y. Crowell, 1971), p. 141.

13. Carol R. Ember and Melvin Ember, *Cultural Anthropology*, 3d ed. (Englewood Cliffs, N.J.: Prentice-Hall, 1981), p. 32.

14. Marvin Harris, *Cows, Pigs, Wars and Witches: The Riddle of Culture* (New York: Vintage Books, 1974).

15. Linda Smircich, "Concepts of Culture and Organizational Analysis," *Administrative Science Quarterly* 28 (1983): 339–58.

16. Bronislaw Malinowski, *A Scientific Theory of Culture* (Chapel Hill: University of North Carolina Press, 1944).

17. A.R. Radcliffe-Brown, *Structure and Function in Primitive Society* (New York: Free Press, 1968).

18. Ward H. Goodenough, *Culture, Language and Society* (Reading, Mass.: Addison-Wesley, 1971).

19. Clifford Geertz, *The Interpretation of Cultures* (New York: Basic Books, 1973).

20. Claude Levi-Strauss, *Structural Anthropology* (Chicago: University of Chicago Press, 1983).

21. E.T. Hall, *Beyond Culture* (Garden City, N.Y.: Anchor Books, 1977), pp. 16–17.

22. J. Child, "Culture, Contingency and Capitalism in the Cross-National Study of Organizations," in L.L. Cummings and B.M. Staw, eds., *Research in Organizational Behavior*, vol. 3 (Greenwich, Conn.: JAI Press, 1981), pp. 303–56.

23. Geert Hofstede, *Culture's Consequences: International Differences in Work-Related Values* (Beverly Hills, Calif.: Sage, 1980).

24. Uma Sekaran and Carol R. Snodgrass, "A Model for Examining Organizational Effectiveness Cross-Culturally," *Advances in International Comparative Management*, vol. 2 (Greenwich, Conn.: JAI Press, 1986), pp. 213, 216–220.

25. Ven Terpstra, *The Cultural Environment of International Business* (Cincinnati: South Western, 1978), p. xvii.

26. Ibid., p. xxii.

27. Geert Hofstede, "Dimensions of National Cultures in Fifty Countries and

Three Regions," in J.B. Deregowski, S. Dziuarawiec, and R.S. Annis, eds., *Explications in Cross-Cultural Psychology* (Lisse, The Netherlands: Soviets and Zeilinger, 1983), pp. 335–55.

28. Child, "Culture, Contingency and Capitalism in the Cross-national Study of Organizations," p. 313.

29. The argument that context-structure relations will be stable across societies is stated as follows:

This hypothesis implicitly rests on the theory that there are imperative, or causal relationships, from the resources of customers, of employees, of materials and finance, etc., and of operating technology of an organization, to its structure, which take effect whatever the surrounding societal differences. (pp. 63–64)

In D.J. Hickson et al., "The Culture-Free Context of Organizational Structure: A Tri-National Comparison," *Sociology* 8 (1974).

30. D.J. Hickson et al., "Grounds for Comparative Organizational Theory: Quicksands or Hard Core?" in C.J. Lammers and D.J. Hickson, eds., *Organizations Alike and Unlike* (London: Routledge and Kegan Paul, 1979), chap. 2.

31. J.H.K. Inkson, D.J. Hickson, and D.S. Pugh, "Administrative Reduction of Variance in Organization and Behavior: A Comparative Study," in D.S. Pugh and R.L. Payne, eds., *Organizational Behavior in Its Context: The Aston Programme III* (Farnborough, Hants: Sasoon House, 1977), chap. 2.

32. A. Sorge, "Cultured Organization" (discussion paper 80-56, Berlin: International Institute of Management, 1980).

33. Ibid.

34. Sekaran and Snodgrass, "A Model for Examining Organizational Effectiveness Cross-Culturally," pp. 216–20.

35. Rabi S. Bhagat and Sara J. McQuaid, "Role of Subjective Culture in Organizations: A Review and Directions for Future Research," *Journal of Applied Psychology Monograph* (October 1982): 653–85.

36. H.A. Witkin et al., *Psychological Differentiation* (Potomac, Md.: Erlbaum, 1974).

37. H.A. Witkin and J.W. Berry, "Psychological Differentiation in a Cross-Cultural Perspective," *Journal of Cross-Cultural Psychology* 6 (1975): 4–87.

38. L.W. Gruenfeld, "Field Dependence and Field Independence as a Framework for the Study of Task and Social Orientations in Organizational Leadership," in D. Graves, ed., *Management Research: A Cross-Cultural Perspective* (Amsterdam, The Netherlands: Eisener North Holland Biomedical Press, 1973).

39. A. Inkeles and D.H. Smith, *Becoming Modern: Individual Change in Six Developing Countries* (Boston: Harvard University Press, 1974).

40. Simcha Ronen and Oded Shenkar, "Clustering Countries on Attitudinal Dimensions: A Review and Synthesis," *Academy of Management Review* 10, no. 3 (1985): 435–54.

41. Peter Blunt, "Techno and Ethnocentrism in Organization Studies: Comment and Speculation Prompted by Ronen and Shenkar," *Academy of Management Review* 11, no. 4 (1986): 857-59.

42. J.W. Atkinson, "Motivational Determinants of Risk Taking Behavior," *Psychological Review* 64 (1957): 359–72.

43. D.C. McClelland, *The Achieving Society* (Princeton, N.J.: Van Nostrand, 1961).

44. P.C. Smith, L.M. Kendal, and C.L. Hulin, *The Measurement of Satisfaction in Work and Retirement: A Strategy for the Study of Attitudes* (Chicago: Rand McNally, 1965).

45. J.C. Adam, "Toward an Understanding of Inequity," *Journal of Abnormal and Social Psychology* 67 (1963): 422–36.

46. A. Maslow, *Motivation and Personality* (New York: Harper and Row, 1954).

47. F. Sahili, "Determinants of Achievement Motivation for Women in Developing Countries," *Journal of Vocational Behavior* 14 (1974): 297–305.

48. H. Soliman, "Motivation-Hygiene Theory of Job Satisfaction: An Empirical Investigation and an Attempt to Reconcile Both the One-and-Two Factor Theories of Job Attitudes," *Journal of Applied Psychology* 54 (1970): 452–61.

49. Ibid.

50. F. Herzberg, B. Mausner, and B. Snyderman, *The Motivation to Work* (New York: Wiley, 1959).

51. C.L. Hulin and M.R. Blood, "Job Enlargement, Individual Differences and Worker Responses," *Psychological Bulletin* 69 (1968): 41–55.

52. William J. Violet, "The Development of International Accounting Standards: An Anthropological Perspective," *International Journal of Accounting Education and Research* (Spring 1983): 1–13.

53. Geert Hofstede, "The Cultural Context of Accounting," in B.E. Cushing, ed., *Accounting and Culture* (Sarasota, Fla.: American Accounting Association, 1987), pp. 1–11.

54. J. Acheson, "Accounting Concepts and Economic Opportunities in a Tarascon Village: Emic and Etic Views," *Human Organization* (Spring 1972): 83–91.

55. G. Chevalier, "Should Accounting Practices Be Universal?" *Canadian Chartered Accountant Magazine* (July 1977): 47-50.

56. L.S. Chang and K.S. Most, "An International Comparison of Investor Uses of Financial Statements," *International Journal of Accounting Education and Research* (Fall 1981): 43–60.

57. A. Belkaoui, A. Kahl, and J. Peyrard, "Information Needs of Financial Analysts: An International Comparison," *International Journal of Accounting Education and Research* (Fall 1977): 19–27.

58. C.W. Nobes, "A Judgmental International Classification of Financial Reporting Practices," *Journal of Business Finance and Accounting* (Spring 1983): 1–19.

59. C.W. Mueller, *International Classification of Financial Reporting* (New York: Croom Helm, 1984).

60. S.S. Zeff, *Forging Accounting Principles in Five Countries: A History and an Analysis of Freud* (Houston: Stipes, 1972).

61. L.H. Radebaugh, "Environmental Factors Influencing the Development of Accounting Objectives, Standards and Practices in Press," *International Journal of Accounting Education and Research* (Fall 1985): 6–16.

62. C.W. Nobes, *International Classification of Financial Reporting* (New York: Croom Helm, 1984).

63. C.W. Nobes, "A Judgmental International Classification of Financial Reporting Practices," pp. 1–19.

64. A. Belkaoui, *International Accounting* (Westport, Conn.: Quorum Books, 1985), chap. 2.

65. A. Belkaoui, *The New Environment in International Accounting* (Westport, Conn.: Quorum Books, 1988).

66. W.G. Frank, "An Empirical Analysis of International Accounting Principles," *Journal of Accounting Research* (Fall 1979): 593–605.

67. M.H.B. Perera and M.R. Mathews, "The Interrelationship of Culture and Accounting with Particular References to Social Accounting," *Advances in International Accounting* (forthcoming).

68. R.D. Nair and W.G. Frank, "The Impact of Disclosure and Measurement Practices on International Accounting Classifications," *The Accounting Review* (July 1980): 426–45.

69. R.C. Da Costa, J.C. Bourgeois, and W.M. Lawson, "A Classification of International Financial Accounting Practices," *International Journal of Accounting, Education and Research* (Spring 1978): 73–85.

70. P.S. Goodrich, "Accounting and Political Systems" (discussion paper no. 109, School of Economic Studies, University of Leeds, 1982).

71. A. Belkaoui, "Economic, Political and Civil Indicators and Reporting and Disclosure Adequacy: Empirical Investigations," *Journal of Accounting and Public Policy* (Fall 1983).

72. A. Belkaoui, "Cultural Determinism and Professional Self-Regulation in Accounting," *Research in Accounting Regulation* (forthcoming).

73. A. Belkaoui, "Managerial, Academic and Professional Influences and Disclosure Adequacy: For Empirical Investigation," *Advances in International Accounting* (forthcoming).

74. A. Belkaoui, "Is Disclosure Adequacy a Cultural or Technical Purpose?" (discussion paper, College of Business Administration, University of Illinois at Chicago, 1989).

75. B.L. Jaggi, "Impact of Cultural Environment on Financial Disclosure," *International Journal of Accounting Education and Research* (Spring 1982): 75–84.

76. Talcott Parsons and Edward A. Shils, eds., *Toward a General Theory of Action* (Cambridge, Mass.: Harvard University Press, 1950).

77. Ibid., p. 8.

78. S.J. Gray, "Towards a Theory of Cultural Influence on the Development of Accounting Systems Internationally," *ABACUS* (March 1988): 1–15.

79. Ibid., p. 8.

80. M. Cole, J. Gray, J. Glick, and D. Sharp, *The Cultural Context of Learning and Thinking* (New York: Banc Books, 1971).

81. B.B. Lloyd, *Perception and Cognition: A Cross-Cultural Perspective* (Middlesex, England: Penguin, 1972).

82. H.C. Triandis, R.S. Malpass, and A.R. Davidson, "Psychology and Culture," *Annual Review of Psychology* 24 (1973): 356.

83. J. Kagan, M.M. Haith, and F.J. Morrison, "Memory and Meaning in Two Cultures," *Child Development* 44 (1973): 356.

84. Cole et al., *The Cultural Context of Learning and Thinking.*

85. J. Goodnow, "Problems in Research on Culture and Thought," in D. Ekland and J. Flavell, eds., *Studies in Cognitive Developments* (New York: Oxford University Press, 1969).

86. P.M. Greenfield, "Comparing Dimensional Categorization in Natural and

Artificial Contents: Λ Developmental Study Among the Zimacantecos of Mexico," *Journal of Social Psychology* 93 (1974): 157–71.

87. A.C. Mundy-Castle, "An Experimental Study of Prediction Among Ghancian Children," *Journal of Social Psychology* 73 (1967): 161–68.

88. M. Cole, J. Gray, J. Glick, and D. Sharp, "Some Experimental Studies of Kjello Quantitative Behavior," *Psychonomic Monographs Supplements* 2 (1968): 173–90.

89. D.A. Wagner, "The Development of Short-Term and Incidental Memory: A Cross-Cultural Study," *Child Development* 45 (1974): 389–96.

90. S. Scribner, "Development Aspects of Categorized Recall in a West African Society," *Cognitive Psychology* 6 (1974): 475–94.

91. J.A. Meacham, "Patterns of Memory Abilities in Two Cultures," *Developmental Psychology* 11, no. 1 (1975): 50–53.

92. P.R. Dasen, "Cross-Cultural Piagetian Research: A Summary," *Journal of Cross-Cultural Psychology* 3 (1972): 23–39.

93. P.R. Dasen, "The Influence of Ecology, Culture and European Contact in Cognitive Development in Australian Aborigines," in J. Berry and P. Dasen, eds., *Culture and Cognition: Readings in Cross-Cultural Psychology* (London: Methuen, 1974).

94. P.R. Dasen, "Concrete Operational Development in Three Cultures," *Journal of Cross-Cultural Psychology* 6, no. 2 (1975): 156–72.

95. T. Gladwin, *East Is a Big Bird* (Cambridge, Mass.: Harvard University Press, 1970).

96. J. Littlejohn, "Cultural Relativism," *Anthropological Quarterly* 36 (1963): 1–17.

97. H.A. Witkin et al., *Psychological Differentiation* (New York: Wiley, 1962).

98. S. Biesheuvel, "The Nature of Intelligence: Some Practical Implications of Its Measurement," in J.B. Jeffrey, ed., *Culture and Cognition: Readings in Cross-Cultural Psychology* (London: Methuen, 1974), p. 221.

99. A.G.J. Cryrs, "African Intelligence: A Critical Survey of Cross-Cultural Intelligence Research in Africa South of the Sahara," *Journal of Social Psychology* 57 (1962): 283-301.

100. S. Biesheuvel, "Psychological Tests and Their Applications to Non-European People," in J.B. Jeffrey, ed., *The Yearbook of Education* (London: Evans, 1949).

101. E.T. Abiola, "The Nature of Intelligence in Nigerian Children," *Teacher Education* 6 (1965): 37–58.

102. J.M. Faverge and J.C. Falmagne, "On the Interpretation in Intercultural Psychology: A Page Written in Recognition of the Work Done in This Field by Dr. S. Biesheuvel," *Psychologia Africana* 9 (1962): 22–36.

103. P.E. Vernon, "Administration of Group Intelligence Tests to East African Pupils," *British Journal of Educational Psychology* 37 (1967); part 3, pp. 251–82.

104. M. Cole and J. Bruna, "Cultural Differences and Influences about Psychological Processes," *American Psychologist* 26 (1971): 867–76.

105. J.W. Berry, "Radical Cultural Relativism and the Concept of Intelligence," in J. Berry and P. Dasen, eds., *Culture and Cognition: Readings in Cross-Cultural Psychology* (London: Methuen, 1974).

106. P.E. Vernon, *Intelligence and Cultural Environment* (London: Methuen, 1969), p. 10.

REFERENCES

Abiola, E.T. "The Nature of Intelligence in Nigerian Children." *Teacher Education* 6 (1965): 37–58.

Acheson, J. "Accounting Concepts and Economic Opportunities in a Tarascon Village: Emic and Etic Views." *Human Organization* (Spring 1972): 83–91.

Adam, J.C. "Toward an Understanding of Inequity." *Journal of Abnormal and Social Psychology* 67 (1963): 422–36.

Adler, Nancy. "A Typology of Management Studies Involving Culture." *Journal of International Business Studies* (Fall 1983): 24–47.

Allport, G.W., P.E. Vernon, and Q. Lindzey. *A Study of Values*. Boston: Houghton Mifflin, 1960.

Atkinson, J.W. "Motivational Determinants of Risk Taking Behavior." *Psychological Review* 64 (1957): 359–72.

Belkaoui, A. "Cultural Determinism and Professional Self-Regulation in Accounting." *Research in Accounting Regulation*. Forthcoming.

———. "Managerial, Academic and Professional Influences and Disclosure Adequacy: For Empirical Investigation." *Advances in International Accounting*. Forthcoming.

———. "Is Disclosure Adequacy a Cultural or Technical Purpose?" Discussion paper, College of Business Administration, University of Illinois at Chicago, 1989.

———. *The New Environment in International Accounting*. Westport, Conn.: Quorum Books, 1988.

———. *International Accounting*. Westport, Conn.: Quorum Books, 1985, chap. 2.

———. "Economic, Political and Civil Indicators and Reporting and Disclosure Adequacy: Empirical Investigations." *Journal of Accounting and Public Policy* (Fall 1983).

Belkaoui, A., A. Kahl, and J. Peyrard. "Informational Needs of Financial Analysts: An International Comparison." *International Journal of Accounting Education and Research* (Fall 1977): 19–27.

Benedict, Ruth. *Patterns of Culture*. New York: Houghton Mifflin, 1934.

Berry, J.W. "Introduction to Methodology." In *Handbook of Cross-Cultural Psychology*, vol. 2, edited by H.C. Triandis and J.W. Berry. Boston: Allyn and Bacon, 1980.

———. "Radical Cultural Relativism and the Concept of Intelligence." In *Culture and Cognition: Readings in Cross-Cultural Psychology*, edited by J. Berry and P. Dasen. London: Methuen, 1974.

———. "On Cross-Cultural Comparability." *International Journal of Psychology* 4, no. 2 (1969): 119–28.

Bhagat, Rabi S., and Sara J. McQuaid. "Role of Subjective Culture in Organizations: A Review and Directions for Future Research." *Journal of Applied Psychology Monograph* (October 1982): 653–85.

Biesheuvel, S. "The Nature of Intelligence: Some Practical Implications of Its Measurements." In *Culture and Cognition: Readings in Cross-Cultural Psychology*, edited by J.B. Jeffrey. London: Methuen, 1974.

————. "Psychological Tests and Their Applications to Non-European People." In *The Yearbook of Education*, edited by J.B. Jeffrey. London: Evans, 1949.

Blunt, Peter. "Techno and Ethnocentrism in Organization Studies: Comment and Speculation Prompted by Ronen and Shenkar." *Academy of Management Review* 11, no. 4 (1986): 857-59.

Boas, Franz. *Anthropology and Modern Life*. New York: W.W. Norton, 1928.

Bohannan, Paul. "Rethinking Culture: A Project for Current Anthropologists." *Current Anthropology* 14, no. 4 (October 1973): 357-65.

Chang, L.S., and K.S. Most. "An International Comparison of Investor Uses of Financial Statements." *International Journal of Accounting Education and Research* (Fall 1981): 43-60.

Chevalier, G. "Should Accounting Practices Be Universal?" *Chartered Accounting Magazine* (July 1977): 47-50.

Child, J. "Culture, Contingency and Capitalism in the Cross-National Study of Organizations." In *Research in Organizational Behavior*, vol. 3, edited by L.L. Cummings and B.M. Staw. Greenwich, Conn.: JAI Press, 1981, pp. 303-56.

Cleary, T.A., and T.L. Hilton. "An Investigation of Item Bias." *Educational and Psychological Measurement* 28 (1968): 61-75.

Cole, M., and J. Bruna. "Cultural Differences and Influences about Psychological Processes." *American Psychologist* 26 (1971): 867-76.

Cole, M., J. Gray, J. Glick, and D. Sharp. *The Cultural Context of Learning and Thinking*. New York: Banc Books, 1971.

————. "Some Experimental Studies of Kjello Quantitative Behavior." *Psychonomic Monographs Supplements* 2 (1968): 173-90.

Comte, Auguste. *A General View of Positivism*. London: Rutledge, 1907.

Cronbach, L.J., G.C. Gleser, H. Nanda, and N. Rajaratnam. *The Dependability of Behavioral Measurements*. New York: Wiley, 1972.

Cronbach, L.J., and P.E. Meehl. "Contrast Validity in Psychological Tests." *Psychological Bulletin* 52 (1955): 281-302.

Cryrs, A.G.J. "African Intelligence: A Critical Survey of Cross-Cultural Intelligence Research in Africa South of the Sahara." *Journal of Social Psychology* 57 (1962): 283-301.

Da Costa, R.C., J.C. Bourgeois, and W.M. Lawson. "A Classification of International Financial Accounting Practices." *International Journal of Accounting, Education and Research* (Spring 1978): 73-85.

Darwin, Charles. *The Descent of Man*. New York: H.M. Caldwell, 1874.

Dasen, P.R. "Concrete Operational Development in Three Cultures." *Journal of Cross-Cultural Psychology* 6, no. 2 (1975): 156-72.

————. "The Influence of Ecology, Culture and European Contact in Cognitive Development in Australian Aborigines." In *Culture and Cognition: Readings in Cross-Cultural Psychology*, edited by J. Berry and P. Dasen. London: Methuen, 1974.

————. "Cross-Cultural Piagetian Research: A Summary." *Journal of Cross-Cultural Psychology* 3 (1972): 23-39.

Diderot, Denis. *Pensees FluConsophiques*. Geneva: E. Droz, 1950.

Ember, Carol R., and Melvin Ember. *Cultural Anthropology*, 3d ed. Englewood Cliffs, N.J.: Prentice-Hall, 1981.

Engels, Friedrich. *The Origin of the Family, Private Property and the State*. New York: International, 1979.

Faverge, J.M., and J.C. Falmagne. "On the Interpretation in Intercultural Psy-

chology: A Page Written in Recognition of the Work Done in This Field
by Dr. S. Biesheuvel." *Psychologia Africana* 9 (1962): 22–36.

Ferguson, Adam. *An Eye on the History of Civil Society.* New York: Garland,
1971.

Fons, J.R., and Ype H. Poortinga. "Cross-Cultural Generalization and Universality." *Journal of Cross-Cultural Psychology* (December 1982): 387–408.

Frake, C.O. "Cultural Ecology and Ethnography." In *Language and Cultural Description: Essays by Charles O. Frake,* edited by S.A. Dil. Stanford, Calif.:
Stanford University Press, 1980, pp. 18–25.

Frank, W.G. "An Empirical Analysis of International Accounting Principles."
Journal of Accounting Research (Fall 1979): 593–605.

Geertz, Clifford. *The Interpretation of Cultures.* New York: Basic Books, 1973.

———. "The Impact of the Concept of Culture on the Concept of Man." In *New
Views on the Nature of Man,* edited by J.R. Platt. Chicago: University of
Chicago Press, 1965.

Gladwin, T. *East Is a Big Bird.* Cambridge, Mass.: Harvard University Press, 1970.

Goodenough, Ward H. *Culture, Language and Society.* Reading, Mass.: Addison-
Wesley, 1971.

Goodnow, J. "Problems in Research on Culture and Thought." In *Studies in Cognitive Developments,* edited by D. Ekland and J. Flavell. New York: Oxford
University Press, 1969.

Goodrich, P.S. "Accounting and Political Systems." Discussion paper no. 109,
School of Economic Studies, University of Leeds, 1982.

Gray, S.J. "Towards a Theory of Cultural Influence on the Development of Accounting Systems Internationally." *ABACUS* (March 1988): 1–15.

Greenfield, P.M. "Comparing Dimensional Categorization in Natural and Artificial Contents: A Developmental Study Among the Zimacantecos of Mexico." *Journal of Social Psychology* 93 (1974): 157–71.

Gruenfeld, L.W. "Field Dependence and Field Independence as a Framework for
the Study of Task and Social Orientations in Organizational Leadership."
In *Management Research: A Cross-Cultural Perspective,* edited by D.
Graves. Amsterdam, The Netherlands: Eisener North Holland Biomedical
Press, 1973.

Hall, E.T. *Beyond Culture.* Garden City, N.Y.: Anchor Books, 1977.

Harner, R.J. "Population Pressure and Ten Social Evolutions of Agriculturalists."
South Western Journal of Anthropology 26 (1970): 67–86.

Harris, Marvin. *Cultural Materialism: The Struggle for a Science of Culture.* New
York: Random House, 1979.

———. *Cows, Pigs, Wars and Witches: The Riddles of Culture.* New York: Vintage
Books, 1974.

———. *Culture, Man and Nature.* New York: Thomas Y. Crowell, 1971.

Harris, P.R., and R.T. Moran. *Managing Cultural Differences.* Houston: Cruff,
1979.

Hegel, Georg Wilhelm Friedrich. *Lectures on the Philosophy of World History:
Introduction.* New York: Cambridge University Press, 1975.

Herzberg, F., B. Mausner, and B. Snyderman. *The Motivation to Work.* New York:
Wiley, 1959.

Hickson, D.J., C.R. Hinings, C.J. McMillan, and J.P. Schmitter. "The Culture-Free Context of Organizational Structure: A Tri-National Comparison." *Sociology* 8 (1974): 59–80.

Hickson, D.J., C.J. McMillan, K. Azumi, and P. Horvath. "Grounds for Comparative Organizational Theory: Quicksands or Hard Core?" In *Organizations Alike and Unlike*, edited by C.J. Lammers and D.J. Hickson, chap. 2. London: Routledge and Kegan Paul, 1979.

Hofstede, Geert. "The Cultural Context of Accounting." In *Accounting and Culture*, edited by B.E. Cushing. Sarasota, Fla.: American Accounting Association, 1987, pp. 1–11.

———. "Dimensions of National Cultures in Fifty Countries and Three Regions." In *Explications in Cross-Cultural Psychology*, edited by J.B. Deregowski, S. Dziuarawiec, and R.S. Annis. Lisse, The Netherlands: Soviets and Zeilinger, 1983, pp. 335–55.

———. *Culture's Consequences: International Differences in Work-Related Values.* Beverly Hills, Calif.: Sage, 1980.

Hulin, C.L., and M.R. Blood. "Job Enlargement, Individual Differences and Worker Responses." *Psychological Bulletin* 69 (1968): 41–55.

Inkeles, A., and D.H. Smith. *Becoming Modern: Individual Change in Six Developing Countries.* Boston: Harvard University Press, 1974.

Inkson, J.H.K., D.J. Hickson, and D.S. Pugh. "Administrative Reduction of Variance in Organization and Behavior: A Comparative Study." In *Organizational Behavior in Its Context: The Aston Programme III*, edited by D.S. Pugh and R.L. Payne, chap. 2. Farnborough, Hants: Sasoon House, 1977.

Irvine, S.H., and W.K. Carroll. "Testing and Assessment Across Cultures: Issues in Methodology and Theory." In *Handbook of Cross-Cultural Psychology*, Vol. 2, edited by H.C. Triandis and J.W. Berry. Boston: Allyn and Bacon, 1980.

Jaggi, B.L. "Impact of Cultural Environment on Financial Disclosure." *International Journal of Accounting Education and Research* (Spring 1982): 75–84.

Kagan, J., M.M. Haith, and F.J. Morrison. "Memory and Meaning in Two Cultures." *Child Development* 44 (1973): 356.

Kluckhohn, F.R., and F. Strodtbeck. *Variations in Value Orientations.* Westport, Conn.: Greenwood Press, 1973.

Lennie, R.A. *Culture, Behavior and Personality.* Chicago: Aldine, 1973.

Levi-Strauss, Claude. *Structural Anthropology.* Chicago: University of Chicago Press, 1983.

———. *Le Cru and Le Cuit.* Paris: Pbon, 1964.

Littlejohn, J. "Cultural Relativism." *Anthropological Quarterly* 36 (1963): 1–17.

Lloyd, B.B. *Perception and Cognition: A Cross-Cultural Perspective.* Middlesex, England: Penguin, 1972.

Lonner, Walter J. "The Search for Psychological Universals." In *Handbook of Cross-Cultural Psychology*, edited by H.C. Triandis and W.W. Lambert. Boston: Allyn and Bacon, 1980, pp. 46, 147–48.

McClelland, D.C. *The Achieving Society.* Princeton, N.J.: Van Nostrand, 1961.

Malinowski, Bronislaw. *Argonauts of the Western Pacific.* New York: Dutton, 1950.

———. *A Scientific Theory of Culture.* Chapel Hill: University of North Carolina Press, 1944.

Malthus, Thomas R. *An Essay on the Principle of Population.* London: T. Bensley, 1803.

Marx, Karl. *A Contribution to the Critique of Political Economy.* New York: International, 1970.

———. *Capital.* Chicago: Encyclopedia Britannica, 1955.

Meacham, J.A. "Patterns of Memory Abilities in Two Cultures." *Developmental Psychology* 11, no. 1 (1975): 50–53.

Mead, Margaret. *Coming of Age in Samoa: A Psychological Study of Primitive Youth for Western Civilization.* New York: Morrow, 1961.

Monroe, R.L., and R.H. Monroe. "Perspectives Suggested by Anthropological Data." In *Handbook of Cross-Cultural Psychology*, edited by H.C. Triandis and W.W. Lambert. Boston: Allyn and Bacon, 1980.

Morey, Nancy C., and Fred Luthans. "An Emic Perspective and Ethoscience Methods for Organizational Research." *Academy of Management Review* 9, no. 1 (1984): 27–36.

Morgan, Lewis Henry. *Ancient Society.* New York: Holt, Rinehart and Winston, 1877.

Morris, C. *Varieties of Human Value.* Chicago: University of Chicago Press, 1956.

Mueller, C.W. *International Classification of Financial Reporting.* New York: Croom Helm, 1984.

Mundy-Castle, A.C. "An Experimental Study of Prediction Among Ghancian Children." *Journal of Social Psychology* 73 (1967): 161–68.

Murdock, G.P. "Common Denominator of Cultures." In *The Science of Man in the World Crises*, edited by R. Linten. New York: Columbia University Press, 1945, pp. 12–42.

Nair, R.D., and W.G. Frank. "The Impact of Disclosure and Measurement Practices on International Accounting Classifications." *The Accounting Review* (July 1980): 426–45.

Nobes, C.W. *International Classification of Financial Reporting.* New York: Croom Helm, 1984.

———. "A Judgmental International Classification of Financial Reporting Practices." *Journal of Business Finance and Accounting* (Spring 1983): 1–19.

Parsons, Talcott, and Edward A. Shils, eds. *Toward a General Theory of Action.* Cambridge, Mass.: Harvard University Press, 1950.

Pelto, P.J. *Anthropological Research: The Structures of Inquiring.* New York: Harper and Row, 1970.

Perera, M.H.B., and M.R. Mathews. "The Interrelationship of Culture and Accounting with Particular References to Social Accounting." *Advances in International Accounting.* Forthcoming.

Pike, K.L. *Language in Relation to a Unified Theory of the Structure of Human Behavior.* 2d ed. The Hague: Mouton, 1967.

Radcliffe-Brown, A.R. *Structure and Function in Primitive Society.* London: Cohen and West, 1961; New York: Free Press, 1968.

Radebaugh, L.H. "Environmental Factors Influencing the Development of Accounting Objectives, Standards and Practices in Press." *International Journal of Accounting Education and Research* (Fall 1985): 6–16.

Rokeach, J. *The Nature of Human Values.* New York: Free Press, 1966.

Ronen, Simcha, and Oded Shenkar. "Clustering Countries on Attitudinal Dimensions: A Review and Synthesis." *Academy of Management Review* 10, no. 3 (1985): 435–54.

Sahili, F. "Determinants of Achievement Motivation for Women in Developing Countries." *Journal of Vocational Behavior* 14 (1974): 297–305.

Sarnoff, I. *Society with Tears.* Secaucus, N.J.: Citadel Press, 1966.

Scribner, S. "Development Aspects of Categorized Recall in a West African Society." *Cognitive Psychology* 6 (1974): 475–94.

Sekaran, Uma, and Carol R. Snodgrass. "A Model for Examining Organizational Effectiveness Cross-Culturally." *Advances in International Comparative Management*, vol. 2. Greenwich, Conn.: JAI Press, 1986, pp. 213, 216–20.

Smircich, Linda. "Concepts of Culture and Organizational Analysis." *Administrative Science Quarterly* 28 (1983): 339–58.

Smith, Adam. *An Inquiry into the Nature and Causes of the Wealth of Nations.* London: J. Maynard, 1811.

Smith, P.C., L.M. Kendal, and C.L. Hulin. *The Measurement of Satisfaction in Work and Retirement: A Strategy for the Study of Attitudes.* Chicago: Rand McNally, 1965.

Soliman, H. "Motivation-Hygiene Theory of Job Satisfaction: An Empirical Investigation and an Attempt to Reconcile Both the One-and-Two Factor Theories of Job Attitudes." *Journal of Applied Psychology* 54 (1970): 452–61.

Sorge, A. "Cultured Organization." Discussion paper 80–56. Berlin: International Institute of Management, 1980.

Spencer, Herbert. *Education: Intellectual, Moral and Physical.* New York: D. Appleton, 1961.

Spradley, J.P. *Participant Observation.* New York: Holt, Rinehart and Winston, 1980.

———. *The Ethnographic Interview.* New York: Holt, Rinehart and Winston, 1979.

Spradley, J.P., and D.W. McCurdy. *The Cultural Experience: Ethnography in Complex Society.* Chicago: Science Research Associates, 1978.

Sturtevant, W.C. "Studies in Ethnoscience." In *Transcultural Studies in Cognition*, edited by A.K. Romney and R.G. D'Andrade. American Anthropologist Special Publication, 1964, pp. 99–131.

Terpstra, Ven. *The Cultural Environment of International Business.* Cincinnati: South Western, 1978.

Triandis, H.C. *The Analysis of Subjective Culture.* New York: Wiley, 1972.

Triandis, H.C., and M. Gerardo. "Etic Plus Emic versus Pseudoetic: A Test of a Basic Assumption of Contemporary Cross-Cultural Psychology." *Journal of Cross-Cultural Psychology* 14, no. 4 (1979): 490.

Triandis, H.C., and L.M. Triandis. "A Cross-Cultural Study of Social Distance." *Psychological Monographs* 76, no. 21 (1962): 16–25.

Triandis, H.C., E.E. Davis, and S.I. Takezawa. "Some Determinants of Social Distance among American, German and Japanese Students." *Journal of Personality and Social Psychology* 2 (1965): 540–41.

Triandis, H.C., R.S. Malpass, and A.R. Davidson. "Psychology and Culture." *Annual Review of Psychology* 24 (1973): 356.

Turgot, Anne Robert Jacques. *Reflections on the Formation and Distribution of Rides.* New York: A.M. Welly, 1963.

Van De Vijver, Fons J.R., and Ype H. Poortinga. "Cross-Cultural Generalization and Universality." *Journal of Cross-Cultural Psychology* (December 1982): 405.

Vernon, P.E. *Intelligence and Cultural Environment.* London: Methuen, 1969.

———. "Administration of Group Intelligence Tests to East African Pupils." *British Journal of Educational Psychology* 37 (1967): part 3, pp. 251–82.

Violet, William J. "The Development of International Accounting Standards: An Anthropological Perspective." *International Journal of Accounting Education and Research* (Spring 1983): 1–13.

Wagner, D.A. "The Development of Short-Term and Incidental Memory: A Cross-Cultural Study." *Child Development* 45 (1974): 389–96.

White, Leslie. *The Science of Culture.* New York: Grove Press, 1949.

Witkin, H.A., and J.W. Berry. "Psychological Differentiation in a Cross-Cultural Perspective." *Journal of Cross-Cultural Psychology* 6 (1975): 4–87.

Witkin, H.A., R.B. Dyk, H.F. Faherson, D.R. Goodenough, and S.A. Karp. *Psychological Differentiation.* New York: Wiley, 1962; Potomac, Md.: Erlbaum, 1974.

Zeff, S.S. *Forging Accounting Principles in Five Countries: A History and an Analysis of Freud.* Houston: Stipes, 1972.

APPENDIX 1.1
ACCOUNTING AND LANGUAGE

1.0 INTRODUCTION

The idea that accounting may be viewed as a language has generated various empirical attempts to evaluate the connotative and denotative meanings of accounting constructs. Because it may be viewed as a language, accounting has been researched using the theories and the methods used in the study of language, namely the "Sapir-Whorf" hypothesis of linguistic relativism, sociolinguistics, and psycholinguistics. The objective of this paper is to elaborate on the attempts in the accounting research literature to view accounting as a language and use the theories and methods prevalent in the study of language.

The study of language is discussed in section 2 of this paper. The argument that accounting may be viewed as a language is presented in section 3. Section 4 presents the principle of linguistic relativity as it is systematized in the social sciences and accounting literature. Section 5 covers the empirical research investigating linguistic relativism in accounting. The relevance of sociolinguistics to accounting is discussed in section 6. The impact of bilingualism to concept perception in accounting is presented in section 7.

2.0 THE STUDY OF LANGUAGE

The study of language as a communication form or a cultural form is important for an understanding of human behavior. In general, the study of language has focused primarily on four areas: structural linguistics, developmental psycholinguistics, linguistic relativity, and sociolinguistics (Belkaoui [1978]).

1. Structural linguistics is devoted to the process of acquisition of language and the identification of formal structural properties.
2. Developmental psycholinguistics deals with formulating language acquisition and use as a special instance of a more general cognitive functioning [Chomsky, 1965; Fodor, 1966]. The main objective is to acquire a better understanding of the human thought process by an examination of grammatical organization and transformation.
3. Linguistic relativity deals with the role of language in our conception of the world. In brief, our world view, or Weltanschauung, as speakers of a given language forces us to interpret the world through the unique grammatical forms and categories that the language supplies [Sapir, 1956; Whorf, 1956].
4. Sociolinguistics, or the sociology of language, is concerned with the existence of different linguistic repertoires in a single language associated with

From Ahmed Belkaoui, "Accounting and Language," *Journal of Accounting Literature* 8 (1989): 281-92.

different social strata and corresponding to different social behaviors [Bernstein, 1958]. This is the study of the characteristics of language varieties, the characteristics of the functions, and the characteristics of their speakers as these three constantly interact and change one another within a speech community [Fishman, 1972].

3.0 ACCOUNTING AS A LANGUAGE

It is customary to call accounting a language or, more precisely, the language of business, since it is an important means of communicating information about a business concern. What makes accounting a language? The answer relies on the parallel between accounting and language. Hawes [1975] defines language as follows:

> Man's symbols are not randomly arranged signs which lead to the conceptualization of isolated and discrete referents. Rather, man's symbols are arranged in a systematic or patterned fashion with certain rules governing their usage. This arrangement of symbol is called a language and the rules which influence the patterning and usage of symbols constitute the grammar of the language. [p. 6]

The above definition identifies two components of a language, symbols and grammatical rules. Therefore, the perception of accounting as a language rests on the identification of accounting symbols and rules. Belkaoui [1978] used the following argumentation:

a) The symbols or lexical characteristics of a language are the "meaningful" units or words identifiable in any language. These symbols are linguistic objects used to identify particular concepts. These symbolic representations do exist in accounting. Numbers and words, debit and credits, may be viewed as symbols generally accepted and unique to the accounting discipline [McDonald, 1972].
b) The grammatical rules of a language refer to the syntactical arrangements existing in any given language. Such rules also exist in accounting. They constitute the general set of procedures used for the creation and dissemination of accounting data. They formalize the structure of accounting in the same way as grammar formalizes the inherent structure of natural language [Jain, 1973].

Given the existence of both symbols and rules as major components, accounting may be defined as priori as a language and researched as the basis of the theories and methods used in the study of language.

4.0 THE "SAPIR-WHORF" HYPOTHESIS OF LINGUISTIC RELATIVISM

Anthropologists have always emphazied the study of language in their studies of culture. Sapir [1956] referred to the linguistic symbolism of a given culture. He perceived language as an instrument of thought and communication of thought. In other words, a given language predisposes its users to a distinct belief. All these premises led to the formulation of the principle of linguistic relativity: that language is an active determinant of thought. Similarly, Whorf [1956] maintained that the ways of speaking are indicative of the metaphysics of a culture. Those metaphysics consist of unstated premises which shape the perception and thought of those who participate in that culture and predispose them to a given mode'of perception.

4.1 SYSTEMATIZATION OF THE "SAPIR-WHORF" HYPOTHESIS

Fishman [1960] provided some order and systematization to the "Sapir-Whorf" hypothesis using a four-fold analytic scheme, as shown in exhibit 1. He distinguishes between the two levels of language—lexical and grammatical—and two types of behavior—linguistic and nonlinguistic. They may be described as follows:

Exhibit 1

A Systematic Version of the Whorfian Hypothesis

Data about language characteristics	Data of speaker's behavior	
	Linguistic data	Nonlinguistic data
Lexical characteristics	1	2
Grammatical characteristics	3	4

(a) The lexical level consists of all words composing a language. Languages differ in terms of the number of terms used to describe a phenomenon.
(b) Linguistic behavior refers to a choice among words, whereas nonlinguistic behavior refers to choices among objects.

This last distinction will become clearer with the explanation of each of the cells identified in exhibit 1.

(1) Cell 1 implies a relationship between the lexical properties of a language and the speaker's linguistic behavior. Phenomena are codified differently in each language. What requires a highly differentiated codification in one language is minimally codified in another language. So, the linguistic behavior or choice of words for a particular phenomenon will be different from one language to another. For example, there are different terms for horses among speakers of Arabic and different terms for snow among speakers of Eskimo.

(2) Cell 2 implies a relationship between lexical properties of a language and the nonlinguistic behavior of the users of a language. It assumes that speakers of a language who make certain lexical distinctions will be able to perform certain nonlinguistic tasks better and more rapidly than the speakers of languages who do not make these lexical distinctions [Brown and Lenneberg, 1954; Lenneberg, 1973; Lantz and Steffre, 1953].

(3) Cell 3 implies a relationship between the grammatical characteristics and linguistic behavior. It assumes that the speakers of one language who use specific grammatical rules are predisposed to a world view different from the speakers of another language [Hoijer, 1951; Ervin-Tripp, 1969].

(4) Cell 4 implies a relationship between grammatical characteristics and nonlinguistic behavior. For example, Carroll and Casagrande [1958] attempted to evaluate whether the speakers of a language such as Navaho who code for color, shape and size in the same verb will classify objects differently from the speakers of language who only code for tense, person, and number in their verbs, as in English. They found that the Navaho-dominant Navahos made object choice as predicted by the grammatical verb more often than did the English-dominant Navahos.

4.2 SYSTEMATIZATION OF LINGUISTIC RELATIVISM IN ACCOUNTING

To accomplish the systematization, a differentiation is made in terms of the different characteristics of accounting language and the different data of congnitive behavior. The characteristics of accounting language have already being defined as the symbolic representations and the manipulation rules. The data of cognitive behavior in accounting refer to the user's behavior, which could be either linguistic or nonlinguistic. The systematization proposed by Belkaoui [1978] consisted of a four-fold analytical scheme as portrayed in exhibit 2. The cells are explained as follows:

Exhibit 2

Propositions of Linguistic Relativism in Accounting

Data about accounting characteristics	Data of user's behavior	
	Linguistic behavior	Nonlinguistic behavior
Symbolic representation	1	1
Manipulation rules	3	4

(1) Cell 1 involves the relationship between the symbolic representations of accounting and the linguistic behavior of users. The codification structure in accounting is more differentiated than in ordinary English, leading to a

different linguistic behavior of users. The first level of the Whorfian in accounting may be expressed as follows:

> The users that make certain lexical distinctions in accounting are enabled to talk and/or solve problems that cannot be easily solved by users that do not. [Belkaoui, 1978, p. 103]

It may be used as a conceptual justification for most studies evaluating the semantic meaning of accounting concepts or content [Oliver, 1974; Haried, 1973].

(2) Cell 2 involves the relationship between the symbolic representations of accounting and the nonlinguistic behavior of users. In other words, it may be conjectured that phenomena or concepts which are highly codified in accounting will be recalled and responded to more often than those less highly codified concepts. This second level of the Whorfian hypothesis in accounting was expressed as follows:

> The users that make certain lexical distinctions in accounting are enabled to perform (nonlinguistic) tasks more readily or completely than those that do not. [Belkaoui, 1978, p.103]

This proposition may be used as a theoretical net for those studies evaluating the impact of accounting content (extent of codification) on the user's decision making. For example, Abdel-Khalik [1973] reports on an empirical study concerning the stipulation that detailed financial information is more useful for lending decision making. Although his results support imputing a higher utility for detailed data only under certain conditions, they are conceptually justifiable under the second Whorfian hypothesis in the sense that the extent of aggregation (or codification) of data implies a different utility and a different nonlinguistic behavior.

(3) Cell 3 involves the relationship between the accounting manipulation rules and linguistic behavior. This third level of the Whorfian hypothesis in accounting was expressed as follows:

> The users that possess the accounting (grammatical) rules are predisposed to different managerial styles or emphases than those that do not. [Belkaoui, 1978, p.103]

Such a proposition could accomodate findings on the differences of common stock perception and preferences arising from the use of alternative accounting techniques [Green and Maheshwari, 1969; Belkaoui and Cousineau, 1977].

(4) Cell 4 involves the relationship between the accounting manipulation rules and nonlinguistic behavior. The fourth level of the Whorfian hypothesis was expressed as follows:

> The accounting techniques may tend to facilitate or render more difficult various (nonlinguistic) managerial behaviors on the part of users. [Belkaoui, 1978, p.103]

The proposition may be used as a theoretical net for the numerous studies evaluating the impact of alternative accounting methods on the user's decision making [Dyckman, Gibbins, and Swieringa, 1978; Belkaoui, 1980a].

5.0 ACCOUNTING RESEARCH IN LINGUISTIC RELATIVITY

Most empirical research investigated the role of accounting as a language and a vehicle of communication without explicit reference to the linguistic relativity hypothesis and by focusing on the connotative meaning of accounting constructs. All types of accounting constructs are assumed to have connotative as well as denotative meanings. The denotative meaning of a construct implies the communication of an objective description of the construct. The connotative meaning implies the communication of a subjective attitude or emotion about the construct. There are, therefore, positive and negative connotations of accounting constructs.

Haried [1972], in a first study, investigated the semantic dimensions of financial statements using the semantic differential technique developed by Osgood, Suci, and Tannenbaum [1957] to measure connotative meanings. In a second study, Haried [1973] reported on the use of a second technique, the antecedent-consequent method developed by Triandis and Kilty [1968] to measure denotative meanings. The antecedent-consequent techniques were found to be useful in examining semantic problems in external accounting communications, but the semantic differential structure within which meaning in accounting was held was different from the standard structure proposed by Osgood, Suci, and Tannenbaum [1957]. Houghton [1988] made a critical analysis of Haried's [1973] own data and showed that (1) the structure within which accounting meaning is held is largely consistent with the seminal work of Osgood, Suci, and Tannenbaum [1957]; and (2) the measured meaning of accounting concepts within that structure is consistent with expectations.

The other studies, however, relied on the semantic differential technique. First, Oliver [1974] used it to measure the semantic meaning of eight selected important accounting concepts using seven selected professional groups involved in the production and use of accounting data to obtain information concerning the relative communication among and between groups. His findings showed a highly significant difference in meanings on six of the eight concepts among the seven professional groups and a major role of the academicians in causing the lack of communications. Second, Flamholtz and Cooke [1978] used the area of human resource accounting as a vehicle for the study of the role of connotative meaning in the process of change in accounting. They also relied on the semantic differential to identify the dimensions of selected traditional and human resource accounting constructs and position these constructs in a semantic space. The results showed the presence of two clusters of constructs: the traditional and the nontraditional. It was then argued that a "semantic halo effect" differentiates between the connotative meaning of traditional and nontraditional accounting constructs, which may explain resistance to accounting innovations such as human resource accounting or socioeconomic accounting. Third, Houghton [1987] also used the semantic differential technique to examine the connotative meaning (and the cognitive structure within which that meaning is held) of "true and fair view" from the point of view of both accountants and private (noninstitutional) shareholders. Significant differences were found between the responses given by accountants and private shareholders. In addition, the factor of cognitive structure in the "expert" accounting groups was seen to be more complex than in private shareholders.

Two studies relied on a psycholinguistic technique, the Cloze procedure. As defined by its creator. Cloze is a "method of intercepting a message from a transmitter (writer or speaker), mutilating its language patterns by deleting parts, and so administering it to receivers (readers or listeners) that their attempts to make patterns whole again potentially yield a considerable number of Cloze units" [Taylor, 1953, p. 416]. In a first study, Adelberg [1979] used the Cloze procedure to measure the understandability of various accounting communications. Empirical evidence showed that differential understandability exists across some, but not all, (1) financial report preparers, (2) financial report messages, and (3) financial report users. It also showed that (1) users do not understand well accounting policies, footnotes, and managements' analyses of operations; and (2) narrative disclosures are not well understood by commercial bank loan officers. In a second study, Adelberg [1982] used the Cloze procedure to empirically evaluate the communication of authoritative pronouncements in accounting. It showed that communication problems do not exist with either authoritative bodies or classes of accountants but do exist with two of the fifteen authoritative pronouncements tested.

All these empirical studies investigating the connotative meanings of accounting concepts focused essentially on the application of methodological techniques like the semantic differential, the antecedent-consequent method, and the Cloze procedure, and failed to integrate and explain their findings using any of the four Whorfian hypotheses. Testing of the four linguistic relativism hypotheses in accounting remains to be done.

6.0 RELEVANCE OF SOCIOLINGUISTICS TO ACCOUNTING

The role of language in defining communities and social relationships is the realm of sociolinguistics. Sociolinguistics assumes that the socialization of individual consciousness and the social molding of personality are largely determined by language [Bernstein, 1958]. The discipline deals with the interaction between two aspects of human behavior—the use of language and the social organization of behavior. The focus is on the generally accepted social organization of language usage within speech communities. This focus is known as the descriptive sociology of language and seeks to discover who speaks or writes what linguistic codes, to whom, when, and why. A second focus is conceived with the discovery of the determinants explaining changes in the social organization of language use and behavior. It is known as the dynamic sociology of language. What both foci imply is the existence in any speech community of verbal varieties of languages or "verbal repertoires." Thus, the sociology of language attempts to explain the underlying causes of the verbal repertoires of a given speech community. The implication of the above statement is that within each language there are linguistic codes which play an important role as a mediator of the perceptual cognitive processes in defining the social environment [Bernstein, 1958; Schatzman and Strauss, 1955; Ervin-Tripp, 1969; Whiteman and Deutsch, 1968].

Relating this to accounting, Belkaoui [1980b] showed that various professional affiliations in accounting create different linguistic repertoires or codes for intragroup communications and/or intergroup communications which lead to a differential understanding of accounting and social relationships. Specifically, a selected set of accounting concepts was subjected to analysis using multidimensional scaling techniques to evaluate the intergroup perceptual differences among three groups of users. A sociolinguistic construct was used to justify the possible lack of consensus on the meaning of accounting concepts. The dimensions of the common perceptual space was identified. They were labeled as conjunctive, relational, and disjunctive by analogy to the process of concept formation. The sociolinguistic thesis was verified for both the conjunctive and the disjunctive concepts. Other issues for future research include: (a) the presence and the nature of the "institutional language" within each accounting professional groups; (b) the presence of a profession-linked linguistic code in the accounting field composed of a "formal language" and a "public language"; and (c) testing whether the public language is understood by users of public data (e.g., financial analysts) and whether the formal language is understood by users of formal data (e.g., students).

Multidimensional scaling techniques were also used by Libby [1979] to investigate bankers' and auditors' perceptions of the message communicated by the audit report. Although not clearly classified, this study falls in the area of sociolinguistics and accounting, since members of different occupational groups are compared as to their perception of an accounting construct, the audit report. Instead, the study argues that the research question can be structured within a "*cognitive conflict paradigm,*" which is based on the lens model.

No disagreements were found as the study reports, surprisingly, that three tests of differences between the auditors' and bankers' perceptions suggested no large differences. This is the only study reporting no difference in the perceptions of connotative meanings of accounting constructs between members of different occupational groups.

7.0 RELEVANCE OF BILINGUALISM TO ACCOUNTING

While accounting is itself a language, its lexical and grammatical characteristics are expressed in each country in the spoken language of that country. Therefore, a problem of communication arises between unilingual accountants from different countries. A second problem may affect bilingual speakers. The two language systems available to bilingual speakers may provide cognitive enrichment or linguistic and perceptual confusion. A third problem facing bilinguals is whether switching from one language to another leads to a better perception. In effect, language switching has been found to be related to higher levels of creativity and cognitive feasibility [Peal and Lambert, 1962], concept formation [Liedke and Nelson, 1968], verbal intelligence [Lambert and Tucker, 1973], and psycholinguistic abilities [Casserly and Edwards, 1973]. The three problems identified can affect the perception of accounting concepts by bilingual and unilingual speakers of languages.

Monti-Belkaoui [1983] conducted an experiment to evaluate the extent of these problems in accounting. The findings of their experiment on accounting concept perception supported the contention that unilingual speakers of separate languages differ from each other and from bilingual speakers in their perception of accounting concepts. Some of the findings also provided support for the contention that language switching may enhance understanding. The evidence suggests that fluency in two languages aids in the uniform acquisition and comprehension of accounting concepts. The need for (and efficacy of) the bilingual international accountant is a research area in need of more attention and empirical validation in the accounting discipline [Belkaoui, 1984, 1989, 1990].

8.0 CONCLUSIONS

A new facet of behavioral accounting is to examine the connotative and denotative meanings of accounting constructs and to investigate the differences in the perception of these constructs by different users and preparers. Most of these attempts were generally characterized by the successful use of the various methodologies used in the study of language, namely semantic differential, antecedent-consequent methods, Cloze procedure, and multidimensional scaling techniques. Some of these attempts went beyond the mere use of these techniques to support the research questions by theoretical models from linguistics; namely the "Sapir-Whorf hypothesis" of linguistic relativism, sociolinguistics, and bilingualism. Much remains to be done as (a) various accounting innovations have different connotative meanings to various professional groups and to various special interest groups; (b) various accounting "institutional" language repertoires arise out of the particular needs and interests of the members of the particular linguistic communities; and (c) the increase in international trade and the efforts to harmonize international accounting create communication perception and expectation problems for speakers of different languages of different cultural backgrounds. Both the profession and academia need to be attuned to these developing problems as they may affect the harmonious growth of the discipline internationally and within any country.

ANNOTATED BIBLIOGRAPHY

Belkaoui, A. 1980. The interprofessional linguistic communication of accounting concepts: An experiment in sociolinguistics. *Journal of Accounting Research* 18, no. 2 (Autumn): 362–74.

The objective of this paper is to explore the application of sociolinguistics to accounting. Three professional groups of users and producers of accounting information were selected in order to determine if there were any differences in their linguistic behavior. A multidimensional scaling model applied to the matrix of similarity judgments enabled the identification of three dimensions and subject saliences. An analysis of variance applied to the individual saliences on each dimension allowed the verification of the sociolinguistic thesis of the differences in the interprofessional linguistic communication of accounting concept.

Flamholtz, E., and E. Cook. 1978. Connotative meaning and its role in accounting change: A field study. *Accounting, Organizations and Society* 3, no. 2: 115–40.

The objective of this paper is to use the area of human resource accounting to study the role of connotative meaning in the process of change in accounting. The semantic differential technique was used. Traditional and nontraditional clusters of constructs were observed. A "semantic halo effect" is suggested to exist as an explanation of the resistance of the subjects to the new accounting constructs of human resource accounting.

Houghton, K. A. 1987. True and fair view: An empirical study of connotative meaning. *Accounting, Organizations and Society* 12, no. 2 (March): 143–52.

The objective of this paper is to empirically examine the connotative meaning (and the cognitive structure within which that meaning is held) of "true and fair view" from the points of view of accountants and "private" (institutional) shareholders. The semantic differential technique was used. The findings show a difference between accountants and shareholders in their perception of the meaning of "true and fair view" as well as differences in their cognitive structures.

Monti-Belkaoui, Janice, and Ahmed Belkaoui. 1983. Bilingualism and the perception of professional concepts. *Journal of Psycholinguistic Research* 12, no. 2: 111–27.

The objective of this paper is to evaluate the intergroup perceptual differences of four experimental groups, made up of unilingual French, unilingual English, and bilingual accounting students. The linguistic relativism thesis provided the research hypotheses on the relationship between language access and usage and accounting concept perception. The multidimensional scaling techniques were applied to the matrix of subjects' similarity judgments on pairs of concepts, thus enabling the identification of three dimensions and subjects' reliances. An analysis of variance of individual saliences on each dimension provided evidence supporting the contention that unilingual speakers of separate languages differ from each other and from bilingual speakers in their perception of accounting concepts.

REFERENCES

Abdel-Khalik, Rashad A. 1973. The effect of aggregating accounting reports on the quality of the lending decision: An empirical investigation. *Empirical Research in Accounting: Selected Studies*: 104–38.

Adelberg, Arthur Harris. 1979. A methodology for measuring the understandability of financial report messages. *Journal of Accounting Research* (Fall): 565–92.

_____. 1982. An empirical evaluation of the communication of authoritative pronouncement in accounting. *Accounting and Finance* (November): 73–94.

Belkaoui, A. 1978. Linguistic relativity in accounting. *Accounting, Organizations and Society* (October): 97–104.

_____. 1980a. The impact of socio-economic accounting statements on the investment decision: An empirical study. *Accounting, Organizations and Society* (September): 263–83.

_____. 1980b. The interprofessional linguistic communication of accounting concepts: An experiment in sociolinguistics. *Journal of Accounting Research* (Autumn): 362–74.

_____. 1984. A test of the linguistic relativity in accounting. *Canadian Journal of Administrative Sciences* (December): 238–55.

Belkaoui, A., 1989. *Behavioral Accounting* (Westport, CT: Greenwood Press).

Belkaoui, A., 1990. *Judgment in International Accounting* (Westport, CT., Greenwood Press). Forthcoming.

Belkaoui, A., and Alain Cousineau. 1977. Accounting information and common stock perception: An application of multidimensional scaling techniques. *The Journal of Business* (July): 334–48.

Bernstein, B. 1958. Some sociological determinants of perception: An enquiry in sub-cultural differences. *Social Psychology*: 454–62.

Brown, R. W. and E. H. Lennenberg, ''A Study in Language and Cognition,'' *Journal of Abnormal and Social Psychology* (1954), pp. 454–462.

Carrol, J. B., and J. B. Casagrade. 1958. The functions of language classification in behavior. In *Readings in Social Psychology*, edited by E. E. Maccoby, T. M. Newcomb, and E. L. Hartley. 3rd ed. (New York: Holt, Rinehart and Winston).

Casserly, M. C., and A. P. Edwards. 1973. *Detrimental effects of grade one bilingualism programs: An exploratory study.* Paper presented at the Annual Conference of the Canadian Psychological Association.

Chomsky, N. 1965. *Aspects of the theory of syntax.* Cambridge, Ma.: MIT Press.

Dyckman, T. R., Gibbins, M., and R. J. Swieringa. 1978. Experimental and survey research in financial accounting: A review and evaluation. In *The Impact of Accounting Research on Practice and Disclosure*, edited by A. R. Abdel-Khalik and T. F. Keller, 48–133. Durham, N.C.: Duke University Press.

Ervin-Tripp, Susan. 1969. Sociolinguistics. In *Advances in experimental social psychology*, edited by L. Berkowitz, 91–165. New York: Academic Press.

Fishman, J. A. 1960. A systematization of the whorfian hypothesis. *Behavioral Science*: 323–39.

_____. 1972. *The sociology of language.* Newbury House Publishers.

Flamholtz, E., and E. Cook. 1978. Connotative meaning and its role in accounting change: A field study. *Accounting, Organizations and Society* (October): 115–40.

Fodor, István. The Problems in the Classification of the African Languages. 1966. Published by The Center for Afro-Asian Research of the Hungarian Academy of Sciences. Budapest, Hungary.

Green, P. E., and A. Maheshwari. 1969. Common stock perception and preference: An application of multidimensional scaling. *Journal of Business* (October): 439–57.

Haried, A. A. 1972. The semantic dimensions of financial statements. *Journal of Accounting Research* (Fall): 376–91.

_____. 1973. Measurement of meaning in financial reports. *Journal of Accounting Research* (Spring): 117–45.

Hawes, Leonard C. 1975. *Pragmatics of analoguing.* Addison-Wesley Publishing Co.

Hoijer, H. 1951. Cultural implications of the Navaho linguistic categories. *Language*: 111–20.

Houghton, K. A. 1987. True and fair view: An empirical study of connotative meaning. *Accounting, Organizations and Society* (March): 143–52.

_____. 1988. The measurement of meaning in accounting: A critical analysis of the principal evidence. *Accounting, Organizations and Society* (February): 263–80.

Jain, Tribhowan N. 1973. Alternative methods of accounting and decision making: A psycholinguistic analysis. *The Accounting Review* (January): 95–104.

Lambert, W. E., and G. R. Tucker. 1973. The benefits of bilingualism. *Psychology Today* (September).

Lantz, D. L., and V. Steffre. 1953. Language and cognition revisited. *Journal of Abnormal and Social Psychology:* 454–62.

Lenneberg, Eric H. 1973. Cognition in ethnolinguistics. *Language:* 463–71.

Libby, Robert. 1979. Bankers' and auditors' perceptions of the message communicated by the audit report. *Journal of Accounting Research* (Spring): 99–122.

Liedke, W. W., and L. D. Nelson. 1968. Concept formation and bilingualism. *Alberta Journal of Educational Research:* 4–20.

McDonald, Daniel. 1972. *Comparative accounting theory.* Addison-Wesley Publishing Co.

Monti-Belkaoui, J., and Ahmed Belkaoui. 1983. Bilingualism and the perception of professional concepts. *Journal of Psycholinguistic Research* 12, no. 2: 111–27.

Oliver, Bruce L. 1974. The semantic differential: A device for measuring the interprofessional communication of selected accounting concepts. *Journal of Accounting Research* (Autumn): 299–316.

Osgood, C. E., G. J. Suci, and P. H. Tannenbaum. 1957. *The measurement of meaning.* Urbana: University of Illinois Press.

Peal, E., and W. Lambert. 1962. The relationship of bilingualism to intelligence. *Psychological Monographs:* 76–84.

Sapir, E. 1956. Culture. In *Language, and Personality: Selected Essays,* edited by D. G. Mandelbaum. Berkeley: University of California Press.

Schatzman, L., and A. Strauss. 1955. Social Class and Modes of a Communication. *American Journal of Sociology:* 329–38.

Taylor, W. 1953. Cloze procedure: A new tool for measuring readability. *Journalism Quarterly* (Fall): 415–33.

Triandis, H. C., and K. M. Kilty. 1968. *Cultural influences of implicative relationship among concepts and the analysis of values.* Group Effectiveness Research Laboratory Report No. 56. Urbana, Ill.: Group Effectiveness Research Laboratory.

Whiteman, M., and M. Deutsch. 1968. Social disadvantage as related to intelligence and language development. In *Social Class, Race and Psychological Development,* edited by M. Deutsch, I. Katz, and A. R. Jensen. New York: Holt, Rinehart and Winston.

Whorf, B. L. 1956. *Language, thought and reality: Selected writings.* Cambridge, Ma.: MIT Press.

2

Cultural Determinism and the Perception of Accounting Concepts

INTRODUCTION

Culture has been considered an important environment factor influencing the accounting system of a country.[1,2] It was also argued that (1) accounting is in fact determined by culture,[3] and (2) the lack of consensus across different countries as to what represents proper accounting methods results because its purpose is cultural, not technical.[4] These arguments represent an acceptance of a cultural determinism in accounting whereby the culture of a given country determines the choice of its accounting techniques and the perception of its various accounting phenomena. This chapter investigates the hypothesis that accountants from different cultural groups will have different perceptions of accounting phenomena.

While several previous empirical and conceptual studies have examined the impact of national culture on accounting, [5-12] this chapter introduces a cognitive perspective to explain the different perceptions of accounting concepts by participants from different groups. In what follows the accounting concepts are identified, followed by the theoretical justification for the experiment. The results of the experiment are then presented.

Portions of this chapter have been adapted with permission from Ahmed Riahi-Belkaoui and R.D. Picur, "Cultural Determinism and the Perception of Accounting Concepts," *The International Journal of Accounting* 26 (1991), pp. 118-30.

THE ACCOUNTING CONCEPTS

The development of the postulates, theoretical concepts, and principles of accounting has always been one of accounting's most challenging and difficult tasks.

Some confusion may be avoided by considering the formulation of the structure of accounting theory as a deductive, interactive process in which the objectives of accounting provide the basis for both the postulates and the theoretical concepts from which the techniques are derived. We begin with the following definitions.

1. The *accounting postulates* are self-evident statements or axioms, generally accepted by virtue of their conformity to the objectives of financial statements, that portray the economic, political, sociological, and legal environments in which accounting must operate.
2. The *theoretical concepts* of accounting are also self-evident statements or axioms, also generally accepted by virtue of their conformity to the objectives of financial statements, that portray the nature of accounting entities operating in a free economy characterized by private ownership of property.
3. The *accounting principles* are general decision rules, derived from both the objectives and the theoretical concepts of accounting, that govern the development of accounting techniques.

The Accounting Postulates

The accounting postulates include the entity postulate, the going-concern postulate, the unit-of-measure postulate, and the accounting-period postulate.

The Entity Postulate

The entity postulate holds that an enterprise is an accounting unit separate and distinct from its owners and other firms. The postulate defines that accountant's area of interest and limits the number of objects, events, and events attributes that are to be included in financial statements. The postulate enables the accountant to distinguish between business and personal transactions: the accountant is to report the transactions of the enterprise, rather than the transactions of the enterprise's owners. The postulate also recognizes the fiduciary responsibility of management to stockholders. The entity concept applies to partnerships, sole proprietorships, corporations (incorporated and unincorporated), and small and large enterprises. It may also apply to a segment of a firm (such as a division) or to several firms (such as a consolidation of interrelated firms).

The Going-Concern Postulate

The going-concern, or continuity postulate, holds that the business entity will continue its operations long enough to realize its projects, commitments, and ongoing activities. The postulate assumes either that the entity is not expected to be liquidated in the foreseeable future or that the entity will continue for an indefinite period of time. Such a hypothesis of stability reflects the expectations of all parties interested in the entity. Thus, the financial statements provide a tentative view of the financial situation of the firm and are only part of a series of continuous reports. Except for the case of liquidation, the user will interpret the information as computed on the basis of the assumption of the continuity of the firm. Accordingly, if an entity has a limited life, the corresponding reports will specify the terminal data and the nature of the liquidation.

The Unit-of-Measure Postulate

A unit of exchange and of measurement is necessary to account for the transactions of firms in a uniform manner. The common denominator chosen in accounting is the *monetary unit*. The exchangeability of goods, services, and capital is measured in terms of money. The unit-of-measure postulate holds that accounting is a measurement and communication process of the activities of the firm that are measurable in monetary terms.

The Accounting-Period Postulate

Although the going-concern postulate holds that the firm will exist for an indefinite period of time, users require a variety of information about the financial position and performance of a firm to make short-term decisions. In response to this constraint imposed by the user environment, the accounting-period postulate holds that financial reports depicting changes in the wealth of a firm should be disclosed periodically. The duration of the period may vary, but income-tax laws, which require income determination on an annual basis, and traditional business practices result in a normal period of a year. Although most companies use an accounting period that corresponds to the calendar year, some companies use a fiscal or a "natural" business year. When the business cycle does not correspond to the calendar year, it is more meaningful to end the accounting period when the business activity has reached its lowest point. Due to the need for more timely, relevant, and frequent information, most companies also issue interim reports that provide financial information on a quarterly or a monthly basis. Empirical studies on stock market reactions to the issuance of interim reports and their impact on users' investment decisions indicate the usefulness of interim reports. To ensure the credibility of interim reports, the Accounting Principles Board issued APB Opinion No. 28, which requires interim reports to be based on the same accounting principles and practices employed in the preparation of annual reports.

The Theoretical Concepts

The theoretical concepts include the proprietary theory, the entity theory, and the fund theory.

The Proprietary Theory

According to the proprietary theory, the entity is the "agent, representative or arrangement through which the individual entrepreneurs or shareholders operate." That the viewpoint of the proprietor group is the center of interest is reflected in the ways in which accounting records are kept and financial statements are prepared. The primary objective of the proprietary theory is the determination and analysis of the proprietor's *net worth*. Accordingly, the accounting equation is

$$\text{Assets} - \text{Liabilities} = \text{Proprietor's Equity}$$

In other words, the proprietor owns the assets and the liabilities. If the liabilities may be considered negative assets, the proprietary theory may be said to be "centered" and, consequently, balance-sheet oriented. Assets are valued and balance sheets are prepared to measure the changes in the proprietary interest or wealth. Revenues and expenses are considered to be increases or decreases, respectively, in proprietorship that do not result from proprietary investments or capital withdrawals by the proprietor. Thus, net income on debt and corporate income taxes are expenses; dividends are withdrawals of capital.

The Entity Theory

The entity theory views the entity as something separate and distinct from those who provide capital to the entity. Simply stated, the business unit, rather than the proprietor, is the center of accounting interest. The business unit owns the resources of the enterprise and is liable to both the claims of the owners and the claims of the creditors. Accordingly, the accounting equation is

$$\text{Assets} = \text{Equities}$$

or

$$\text{Assets} = \text{Liabilities} + \text{Stockholders' Equity}$$

Assets are rights accruing to the entity; equities represent sources of the assets and consist of liabilities and the stockholders' equity. Both the creditors and the stockholders are equity holders, although they have different rights with respect to income, risk control, and liquidation. Thus, income earned is the property of the entity until it is distributed as dividends to the shareholders. Because the business unit is held responsible for meeting the claims of the equity holders, the entity theory is said to be "income-centered" and, consequently, income-statement oriented. Accountability to the equity holders is accomplished by measuring the operating and financial performances of the firm. Accordingly, income is an increase in the stockholders' equity after the claims of other equity holders (for example, interest on long-term debt and income taxes) are met. The increase in the stockholders' equity is considered income to the stockholders only if a dividend is declared. Similarly, undistributed profits remain the property of the entity because they represent the corporation's proprietary equity in itself. Note that strict adherence to the entity theory dictates that income taxes and interest on debt be considered distributions of income rather than expenses. The general belief and the interpretation of the entity theory, however, is that interest and income taxes are expenses.

The Fund Theory

Under the fund theory, the basis of accounting is neither the proprietor nor the entity, but a group of assets and related obligations and restrictions, called a fund, that governs the use of the assets. Thus, the fund theory views the business unit as consisting of economic resources (funds) and related obligations and restrictions regarding the use of these resources. The accounting equation is

$$\text{Assets} = \text{Restrictions of Assets}$$

The accounting unit is defined in terms of assets and the uses to which these assets are committed. Liabilities represent a series of legal and economic restrictions on the use of the assets. The fund theory is therefore "asset-centered" in the sense that its primary focus is on the administration and the appropriate use of assets. Instead of the balance sheet or the financial statement, the statement of sources and uses of funds is the primary objective of financial reporting. This statement reflects the conduct of the operations of the firm in terms of sources and dispositions of funds.

The Accounting Principles

The accounting principles include the cost principle, the revenue principle, the matching principle, the objectivity principle, the consistency principle, the full disclosure principle, the conservatism principle, the materiality principle, and the comparability principle.

The Cost Principle

According to the cost principle, the *acquisition cost* or *historical cost* is the appropriate valuation basis for recognition of the acquisition of all goods and services, expenses, costs, and equities. In other words, an item is valued at the exchange price at the date of acquisition and is recorded in the financial statements at that value or an amortized portion of that value.

Cost represents the exchange price of or the monetary consideration given for the acquisition of goods or services. If the consideration comprises nonmonetary assets, the exchange price is the cash equivalent of the assets or services given up. The cost principle is equally applicable to the measurement of liabilities and capital transactions. The cost principle may be justified in terms of both its objectivity and the going-concern postulate. First, acquisition cost is objective, verifiable information. Second, the going-concern postulate assumes that the entity will continue its activities indefinitely, thereby eliminating the necessity of using current values or liquidation values for asset valuation.

The Revenue Principle

The revenue principle specifies (1) the nature of the components of revenue, (2) the measurement of revenue, and (3) the timing of revenue recognition. In general, revenue is recognized on an accrual basis or on a critical-event basis.

The *accrual basis* for revenue recognition may imply that revenue should be reported during production (in which case the profit may be computed proportionally to the work completed or the service performed), at the end of production, on sale of goods, or on collection of sale. Revenue is generally recognized during production in the following situations:

1. Rent, interest, and commission revenue are recognized as earned, given the existence of a prior agreement or a contract specifying the gradual increase in the claim against the customer.

2. An individual or a group rendering professional or similar services might better use an accrual basis for the recognition of revenue, given that the nature of the claim against the customer is a function of the proportion of services rendered.

3. Revenues on long-term contracts are recognized on the basis of the progress of construction or the "percentage of completion." The percentage of completion is computed as either (a) the engineering estimates of the work performed to date compared with the total work to be completed in terms of the contract or (b) the total costs incurred to date compared with the total costs estimated for the total project in the contract.

4. Revenues on "cost plus fixed-fee contracts" are better recognized on the accrual basis.

5. Asset changes due to accretion give rise to revenue (for example, when liquor or wines age, timber grows, or livestock matures). Although a transaction must occur before revenue is recognized in these examples, accretion revenue is based on comparative inventory valuations.

The *critical-event basis* for revenue recognition is triggered by a crucial event in the operating cycle. That event may be (1) the time of sale, (2) the completion of production, or (3) the receipt of payment subsequent to sale.

The *sales basis* for the recognition of revenue is justified because (1) the price of the product is then known with certainty, (2) the exchange has been finalized by delivery of goods, leading to an objective knowledge of the costs incurred, and (3) in terms of realization, a sale constitutes a crucial event.

The *completion-of-production basis* for the recognition of revenue is justified when a stable market and a stable price exist for a standard commodity. The production process rather than the sale therefore constitutes the crucial event for the recognition of revenue. This rule is primarily applicable to "precious metals that have a fixed selling price and insignificant market prices." The completion-of-production treatment is appropriate for gold, silver, and other precious metals and may also be appropriate for agricultural and mineral products that meet the required criteria.

The *payment basis* for the recognition of revenue is justified when the sale will be made and when a reasonably accurate valuation cannot be placed on the product to be transferred. This method, which amounts to a mere deferral of revenue, is primarily identified with the "installment method" of recognizing revenue.

The Matching Principle

The matching principle holds that expenses should be recognized in the same period as the associated revenues; that is, revenues are recognized in a given period according to the revenue principle, and the related expenses are then recognized. The association is best accomplished when it reflects the cause-and-effect relationship between costs and revenues. Operationally, it consists of a two-stage process for accounting for expenses. First, costs are capitalized as assets representing bundles of service potentials or benefits. Second, each asset is written off as an expense to recognize the revenue during this period. Thus, accrual accounting rather than cash accounting is implied by the matching principle in terms of capitalization and allocation.

The association between revenues and expenses depends on one of four criteria:

1. Direct matching of expired costs with a revenue (for example, cost of goods sold matched with related sale).
2. Direct matching of expired cost with the period (for example, president's salary for the period).

3. Allocation of costs over periods benefitted (for example, depreciation).

4. Expensing all other costs in the period incurred, unless it can be shown that they have future benefit (for example, advertising expense).

The Objectivity Principle

The usefulness of financial information depends heavily on the *reliability* of the measurement procedure used. Because ensuring maximum reliability is frequently difficult, accountants have employed the objectivity principle to justify the choice of a measurement or a measurement procedure. The principle of objectivity, however, has been subject to different interpretations:

1. An objective measurement is an "impersonal" measure, in the sense that it is free from the personal bias of the measurers.

2. An objective measurement is a verifiable measurement, in the sense that it is based on an evidence.

3. An objective measurement is the result of a consensus among a given group of observers or measurers. This view also implies that objectivity will depend on the given group of measurers.

4. The size of the dispersion of the measurement distribution may be used as an indicator of the degree of objectivity of a given measurement system.

The Consistency Principle

The consistency principle holds that similar economic events should be recorded and reported in a consistent manner from period to period. The principle implies that the same accounting procedures will be applied to similar items over time. Application of the consistency principle makes financial statements more comparable and more useful. Trends in accounting data and relationships with external factors are more accurately revealed when comparable measurement procedures are used. Similarly, the distortion of income and balance sheet amounts and the possible manipulation of financial statements are avoided by the consistent application of accounting procedures over time. Consistency is therefore a user constraint intended to facilitate the user's decision by ensuring the comparable presentation of the financial statements of a given firm over time, thereby enhancing the utility of the statements. Consistency is a major concern of accountants when auditing financial statements. In the standards opinion, the certified public accountant recognizes the consistency principle by noting whether or not the financial statements have been prepared in conformity with generally accepted accounting principles applied on a basis "consistent with that of the preceding year."

The consistency principle does not preclude a firm changing accounting procedures when this is justified by changing circumstances, or if the alternative procedure is preferable (*the rule of preferability*). According to APB Opinion No. 20, changes that justify a change in procedure are (1) a change in accounting principle, (2) a change in accounting estimate, or (3) a change in reporting entity. These changes are to be reflected in the accounts and reported in the financial statements *retroactively* for a change in accounting entity, *prospectively* for a change in accounting estimate, and *generally* and *currently* for a change in accounting principle.

The Full Disclosure Principle

There is a general consensus in accounting that there should be "full," "fair," and "adequate" disclosure of accounting data. *Full disclosure* requires that financial statements be designed and prepared to portray accurately the economic events that have affected the firm for the period and to contain sufficient information to make them useful and not misleading to the average investor. More explicitly, the full disclosure principle implies that no information of substance or of interest to the average investor will be omitted or concealed.

The principle is further reinforced by the various disclosure requirements set forth by the APB Opinions, the FASB Statements, and the SEC Accounting Releases and requirements. Full disclosure is, however, a broad, open-ended construct that leaves several questions unanswered or open to different interpretations. First, what is meant by "full," "fair," and "adequate" disclosure? "Adequate" connotes a minimum set of information to be disclosed; "fair" implies an ethical constraint dictating an equitable treatment of users; and "full" refers to complete and comprehensive presentation of information. Another accepted position is to view "fairness" as the central objective and trade-off point between full and adequate disclosure.

The Conservatism Principle

The conservatism principle is an exception or modifying principle in the sense that it acts as a constraint to the presentation of relevant and reliable accounting data. The conservatism principle holds that when choosing among two or more acceptable accounting techniques, some preference is shown for the option that has the least favorable impact on the stockholders' equity. More specifically, the principle implies that preferably the lowest values of assets and revenues and the highest values of liabilities and expenses should be reported. The conservatism principle therefore dictates that the accountant display a generally pessimistic attitude when choosing accounting techniques for financial reporting. To accomplish the objectives of understanding current income and assets, the conservatism principle may lead to treatments that constitute a departure from acceptable or theoretical approaches. For example, the adoption of the "lower-of-cost-or-market" concept conflicts with the historical principle. Although the LIFO (last in-first out) valuation and accelerated depreciation are generally perceived as counterinflationary measures, they may be viewed as resulting from the adoption of the conservatism principle.

The Materiality Principle

Like conservatism, the materiality principle is an exception or modifying principle. The principle holds that transactions and events having insignificant economic effects may be handled in the most expeditious manner, whether or not they conform to generally accepted accounting principles, and need not be disclosed. Materiality serves as an implicit guide for the accountant in terms of what should be disclosed in the financial reports, enabling the accountant to decide what is not important or what does not matter on the basis of record-keeping cost, accuracy of financial statements, and relevance to the user.

The Comparability Principle

The consistency principle refers to the use of the same procedures for related items by a given firm over time; the uniformity principle refers to the use of the same procedures by different firms. The desired objective is to achieve comparability of financial statements by reducing the diversity created by the use of different accounting procedures by different firms. In fact, a constant debate is taking place over whether flexibility or uniformity should prevail in accounting and financial reporting. The principal supports for uniformity are the claims that it would:

1. Reduce the diverse use of accounting procedures and the inadequacies of accounting practices.
2. Allow meaningful comparisons of the financial statements of different firms.
3. Restore the confidence of users in the financial statements.
4. Lead to governmental intervention and regulation of accounting practices.

The main supports for flexibility are the claims that:

1. The use of uniform accounting procedures to represent the same item occurring in many cases poses the risk of concealing important differences among cases.
2. Comparability is a utopian goal.
3. "Differences in circumstances" or "circumstantial variables" call for different treatments, so that corporate reporting can respond to circumstances in which transactions and events occur.

The implicit objective of both uniformity and flexibility is to protect the user and to present the user with meaningful data. Both principles fail due to their extreme positions on the issue of financial reporting. Uniformity does not lead to comparability—an admittedly unfeasible goal. Flexibility evidently leads to confusion and mistrust. A trade-off solution may be provided by encouraging uniformity by narrowing the diversity of accounting practices and, at the same time, allowing a proper recognition of market and economic events peculiar to a given firm and a given industry by a proper association of certain economic circumstances with related accounting techniques. This middle position calls for an operational definition of "differences in circumstances" and for better guidelines for relating differences in circumstances to various procedures.

THEORETICAL JUSTIFICATION:
A COGNITIVE-CULTURAL PROCESS

A Cognitive View of the Judgment Process

In what follows a model of the judgment/decision process in accounting is proposed as an exercise in social perception and cognition, requiring both formal and implicit judgment. The primary input to this process is an accounting problem or phenomenon that needs to be solved and requires a judgment preceding either a preference or a decision. The model consists of the following steps:

1. Observation of the accounting phenomenon by the decision maker;
2. Schema formation or building of the accounting phenomenon;
3. Schema organization and storage;
4. Attention and recognition process triggered by a stimulus;
5. Retrieval of stored information needed for the judgment/decision;
6. Reconsideration and integration of retrieved information with other available information;
7. The judgment process; and
8. Decision/action (response).

Observation of the Accounting Phenomenon
by the Decision Maker

The decision maker is assumed to have the opportunity to observe the accounting phenomenon. To understand the phenomenon the decision maker may be given some information which is deemed diagnostic. If this information is not provided, the decision maker may seek the information and test available information judged most relevant to the phenomenon. The search behavior may concentrate on these types of available information:

1. Consensus information (how this accounting phenomenon and other accounting phenomena were rated or performed on given dimensions);

2. Distinctiveness information (how this accounting phenomenon was rated or performed on various other dimensions); and

3. Consistency information (how this accounting phenomenon was rated or performed on important dimensions in the past).

Schema Formation or Building of the Accounting Phenomenon

Once the accounting phenomenon has been observed, the relevant information is encoded in the sense that it is categorized on the basis of experience and organized in memory along schemata or knowledge structures. A schema can be simply an update of templates that existed prior to the occurrence of a known accounting phenomenon, or a new template generated by the occurrence of a new accounting phenomenon. In the first case, little ambiguity is assumed to exist, and therefore the encoding follows an automatic process. In the second case, no immediate available schema exists, and a controlled categorization process is triggered to determine which schema is consistent with the dimensions of the accounting phenomenon. Both processes are suggested in the case of the encoding of information or performance appraisal.

Basically, an accounting phenomenon may be categorized, in a given schema, by virtue of its possession of obvious or salient attributes known to the perceiver. When no salient category prototype or schema provides a natural framework, the automatic process is superseded by a controlled process or a consciously monitored process.

The controlled process can be triggered by either a new accounting phenomenon or new features of a known phenomenon that are inconsistent with a previous categorization. In the latter case a recategorization is invoked until the inconsistency is resolved, and a new schema is used to describe the accounting phenomenon, causing a reconstruction of memories about the phenomenon such that memories consistent with the new categorization are more available.

Schema Organization and Storage

After information about a given phenomenon is encoded to form a representation or schema, it is stored and maintained in long-term memory. Basically, a person's episodic memories are personal, while semantic memory is knowledge of words and symbols, their meanings and referent knowledge of the relations among words, and the rules or algorithms for manipulating words, symbols, and the relations among them. Information enters the memory system through the various senses and goes first to the sensory register, whose function is to preserve incoming information long enough for it to be selectively transmitted into the memory system. It is kept there less than a second and is lost either through decay or erasure by overwriting.

The information then goes to the short-term store, "working in memory" where conscious mental processes are performed. It is where consciousness exercises its function. Information can be kept indefinitely here provided that it is given constant attention; if not, it is lost through decay in twenty to thirty seconds.

The information next goes to the long-term store through a conscious or unconscious process, where it can be held indefinitely and often permanently (although it can be lost due to decay or interference of various sorts). The long-term store is assumed to have unlimited capacity. In this multistore model information about the accounting phenomenon moves through different and separate memory systems, ending with a long-term store where semantic information is maintained along meaning-based codes or schemata. It is important to realize at this stage that if the person intends to remember the accounting phenomenon for all time, he/she must perform a different analysis on the input than when his/her intentions are temporary. A person's intention determines whether the storage of the information on the accounting phenomenon is permanent or temporary. A different coding is used: a memory code for permanent storage and a perceptual role for temporary storage.

Attention and Recognition Process Triggered by a Stimulus

Upon observation of a triggering event or stimulus, the schema in the accounting phenomenon is activated. The activation, as a process of detection, search, and attention, can be either a controlled or an automatic processing.

Basically, automatic detection, triggered by the recognition of a stimulus, operates independently of the person's control. Automatic processing is the apprehension of stimuli by the use of previously learned routines that are in the long-term storage.

In these automatic processes, no conscious effort is involved in the search, as well as in demanding attention due to the learned sequence of the elements composing the schemata.

On the other hand, controlled processes involve a temporary activation of novel sequences of processing steps that require attention, use short-term memory, and involve a conscious effort.

It is important to realize that in both processes, the use of schemata for encoding or retrieving information depends on accessibility in memory, where the accessibility of schemata is the probability that they can be activated.

Retrieval of Stored Information Needed for the Judgment/Decision

Either the automatic or controlled search processes activate the appropriate schema for the accounting phenomenon and allow the retrieval of information on the phenomenon. It is, however, the schema, a representation of the phenomenon, that is recalled rather than the actual phenomenon. The effect becomes stronger as the time between observation and recall increases.

Reconsideration and Integration of Retrieved Information with Other Available Information

At this stage the process involves the integration of the information retrieved from memory and other available information into a single evaluation of the accounting phenomenon.

Where familiarity with the phenomenon is present and previously learned routines are retrieved, active integration will not take place. An earlier integration is recalled from past stored output on the phenomenon.

Where the phenomenon presents challenging and novel dimensions and where controlled processes were involved in attention and recognition, a cognitive integration of all the information is required to reach a single evaluation of the accounting phenomenon.

The Judgment Process

The judgment process is the result of the integration process of information and the forming of a single evaluation of the accounting phenomenon if the attention, recognition, and integration processes are the result of controlled processes. The judgment made in this case requires a conscious access to all the mental processes implied in the model. If, however, the attention, retrieval recognition, and integration processes were the result of automatic processes, the judgment is not and will not be conscious. It does not require the conscious use of all the mental processes implied in this model. It is a routine judgment.

Decision/Action (Response)

The final step of the model is the decision or selection of a response to the accounting phenomenon. It is a conscious response preference resulting from the judgment process. It is an output of the judgment process and is clearly influenced by all the mental processes and biases described earlier. As a result, a new schema on the phenomenon will develop that will be part of the knowledge structure or the phenomenon stored in long-term memory.

The move from judgment to decision is a bridging process. It assumes that no obstacles stand in the way.

The decision/action has been investigated in various accounting environments and using various accounting phenomena. It has been found to differ from various normative decision models, including Bayerian decision theory and expected value models.

The bridging process, however, will be influenced by the cognitive steps described in this model as well as by other factors, including the possible consequences of the decision on the accounting phenomenon.

A Cultural View of the Judgment Process

The concept of culture is not monolithic.[13-15] Each of the concepts of "culture" from anthropology created different metaphors and ends in organizational research. Malinowski's functionalism, with its view of culture as an instrument serving human biological and psychological needs, motivated cross-cultural or comparative management research.[16,17] Radcliffe-Brown's structuralism, with its view of culture as an adaptive regulatory mechanism that unites individuals in social structures, motivated research on corporate culture.[18] Goodenough's ethnoscience, with its view of culture as a system of shared cognitions where the human mind generates culture by means of a finite number of rules, motivated research on organizational cognition.[19-21] Geertz's symbolic anthropology, with its view of culture as a system of shared symbols and meanings where symbolic action needs to be interpreted, read, or deciphered in order to be understood, motivated research on organizational symbolism.[22] Finally, Levi-Strauss's structuralism, with its view of culture as a projection of mind's universal unconscious infrastructure, motivated research on unconscious processes and organization.[23]

The interest in this chapter is concept perception; therefore, a cognitive functioning view of culture is adopted to explicate cultural determinism in accounting. Culture is viewed as a system of shared cognitions or a system of knowledge and beliefs, "a unique system for perceiving and organizing materials, phenomena, things, events, behaviors and emotions."[24] It is generated in the human mind "by means of a finite number of rules or means of unconscious logic."[25]

Using the cognitive emphasis, national cultures act as networks of subjective meanings or shared frames of reference that members of each culture share to varying degrees and which, to an external observer, appear to function in a rule-like, or grammar-like manner. Relating this to accounting and the cultural determinism thesis in accounting, we assume that different cultural groups in accounting create different cognitions or systems of knowledge for intracultural communications and/or intercultural communications. These, in turn, lead to a different understanding of accounting relationships. This led to the following research question: "Are the perceptions of accounting concepts, as measured by the individual weights assigned by the participants to the dimensions of a common perceptual space, a function of the cultural group membership?"

Multidimensional scaling techniques are used to evaluate the differences in accounting concept perceptions by participants from different cultural groups within the accounting profession. The presumed differences may be a function of certain psychological, perceptual, and background variables. The variables examined are: (1) the subject's age, (2) his/her academic degree, (3) his/her familiarity with financial statements, (4) the number of years of experience with the CPA firm, and (5) the number of years in the present position.

METHOD

Sample

The choice of subjects in our field experiment was motivated by the need to isolate the impact of national culture on the perception of accounting concepts from the potential impact of organizational culture and linguistic relativism. To control for the impact of organizational culture, respondents were recruited from three offices of the same international Big Six accounting firm, with a strong American orientation in organizational philosophies and policies. To control for the impact of linguistic relativism, the three offices were chosen in three Anglophone cities, namely Chicago, London, and Toronto. Therefore, English-speaking partners or managers from the local offices of a Big Six international firm located in three different national cultures, American, British, and Canadian, were asked to participate in our study and to indicate their perceptions of accounting concepts. The main difference in the subjects that may influence their perception of accounting concepts was the difference in their national culture.

A questionnaire was given to an official at the headquarters of the Big Six firm, who agreed to coordinate the distribution of the questionnaire in the three cities and to return them to the researchers. The official was instructed to include as respondents only the employees of the firm in the three cities who:

1. Were active in the accounting and auditing practice (thus excluding tax and consulting practice as well as administrative and other supporting staff);
2. Have reached the manager or partner level; and
3. Were born in the national culture of the country where the local office is located.

These criteria produced a population of 87 respondents composed of 47 American, 21 British, and 19 Canadian partners or managers.

Research Instrument

Subjects in the three cultural groups were given the same questionnaire, written in English. The questionnaire required subjects to assign similarity judgments to paired sets of twelve concepts. In multidimensional scaling techniques, such similarity judgments are interpreted as "psychological distances," representing a "mental map" through which respondents view pairs of concepts that are "near" each other as similar and pairs of concepts that are "far apart" as dissimilar. If numerical measures are provided for the similarity judgments, multidimensional scaling techniques may be used to construct a "physical" multidimensional map whose interpoint distances closely relate to the input data.

One of the multidimensional scaling techniques used in the study is the TORSCA non-metric scaling routine.[26] Given $n(n-1)/2$ similarity/dissimilarity measures, the TORSCA program first yields a set of orthogonal coordinates for the final configuration and then estimates the dimensionality of the data. The other algorithm used in this study, the INDSCAL model, assumes that all individuals share a common perceptual space but assigns differential weights or salience to the different dimensions of the groups stimulus space. The individual saliences provide an operational measure for an evaluation of the possible inter- and intracultural group perceptual differences.

Both these multidimensional scaling techniques, the TORSCA and INDSCAL models, were applied to individual similarity judgments to estimate the dimensions of the common perceptual space and each respondent's salience. Regression was then used to measure the relation between salience and selected background variables which included the subject's age, the number of years employed in the firm, and the number of years employed in the present position.

Professional Concepts and Experimental Decisions

The twelve concepts used in the study were chosen to reflect two categories of accounting concepts of relevance to accounting theory construction. The terms "going concern," "entity," "stable monetary unit," and "periodicity" represent underlying assumptions of accounting theory, while the terms "cost principle," "revenue principle," "matching principle," "objectivity principle," "consistency principle," "full disclosure principle," "materiality principle" and "conservatism principle" represent generally accepted accounting principles within the profession.[27]

Each of the participants was asked to do the following: (1) provide information on certain background variables; (2) for each of the financial statements assign a familiarity rating ranging from "not familiar" to "extremely familiar"; (3) for each of the pairs of twelve concepts used as stimuli, assign an integer rating on a seven-point scale ranging from "very dissimilar" to "very similar"; and (4) list the criteria used for assigning the similarities.

Procedure

The input to the TORSCA is a single, rank-ordered similarity matrix computed by averaging the cell ranks obtained across all participants. The measure of departure from perfect fit, the "stress of the configuration," is used. As suggested by Kruskai,[28,29] the departure from perfect fit (stress = 0) can be expressed as follows: .025 excellent; .05 good; .10 fair.

The input to the INDSCAL is the $87\times12\times12$ matrix of similarity judgments for all participants. The measure of fit used is the squared correlation in distances (RSQ). The RSQ values are the proportion of variance of the scaled data (disparities) in the partition (row, matrix, or entire data) which is accounted for by their corresponding distances.

Both TORSCA and INDSCAL will yield a set of dimensions of a common configuration that need to be identified. One way to identify the dimensions is the "maximum congruence" method of Miller, Shepard, and Chang.[30] The method correlates the coordinates of the solution with ratings obtained from the respondents on a set of candidate attributes. This method was not used in this study, as the provision of a set of candidate attributes may potentially influence the responses of the subjects in their similarity rating task toward one single way of thinking. The method used in this study was to ask the participants to state in order of importance the criteria used in making their similarity judgments. The rationale is that in assigning similarity ratings among concepts, a process of concept perception is generally used, consisting of either the recognition of shared or linked characteristics in the accounting concepts (stimulus generalization) or the recognition of shared differences (stimulus discrimination). In either case, the process of concept formation results in the grouping of experiences into conceptual classes on the basis of similarities in their characteristics.[31] Hunt and Hovland[32] classified the concepts as being conjunctive, relational, or disjunctive. Conjunctive concepts are perceived as those sharing common perceptual characteristics. Relational concepts are those linked by some fixed relationships. Finally, disjunctive concepts are those concepts which differ on the basis of one or more characteristics.

RESULTS

Preliminary Findings

The use of TORSCA resulted in the average stress indices of .356, .092 and .868 for two, three, and four dimensions, respectively. Based on these results, a "goodness of fit" is provided by three dimensions (stress ≤ .10). Kruskal considered a stress index under .10 to be fair. In addition, Klahr,[33] measuring stress indices from random data, concluded that for twelve stimuli there was only a 5 percent chance that a solution is random, if the stress index is not greater than 0.118. The use of INDSCAL produced an RSQ measure and the three-dimensional solution used in this study.

Identification of Perceptual Dimensions

The participants had indicated the criteria they had used in making their similarity judgments. An examination of the participants' answers revealed a consensus toward assigning similarity judgments on the basis of the existence or absence of common perceptual qualities between each pair of accounting concepts. An examination of the answers showed evidence of a process of concept formation used by the participants. It follows that the three-way concept perception classification is used to identify the three dimensions obtained in the INDSCAL model solution listed in Exhibit 2.1.

An examination of the stimulus configuration in Exhibit 2.1 shows, for example, stable monetary unit and objectivity principle and consistency and materiality on opposite sides of dimension III. Similarly, revenue and cost principles and entity and objectivity are on opposite and equal sides of dimension I. Finally materiality and conservatism and entity and going concern are the same equal side of dimension II. On the basis of these extra-statistical findings, dimension I may be labeled as the relational dimension, dimension II as the conjunctive dimension, and dimension III as the disjunctive dimension.

Intergroup Perceptual Differences

The INDSCAL model provides weights or saliences that each participant assigned to each of the three dimensions. A one-way analysis of variance for the three cultural groups of participants is used to determine if they have different saliences on each of the three dimensions. The results of the analysis of variance are portrayed in Exhibit 2.2. The hypotheses of no differences in the intercultural group perceptual differences is rejected for both the conjunctive and relational dimensions, but not for the disjunctive dimension (at a level of confidence $\alpha = .10$). Basically the different cultural groups in accounting created different cognitions or systems of knowledge for the perception of accounting concepts that share common perceptual characteristics (conjunctive concepts), or that are linked by some fixed relationship (relational concepts). The cognitive structure was not different among the three groups for the accounting concepts that differ on the basis of one or more characteristics (disjunctive concepts). Therefore a partial verification of the cultural determinism hy-

Exhibit 2.1
Accounting Concepts' Salience in Three-Dimensional Space

Accounting Concepts	Salience		
	Dimension 1	Dimension 2	Dimension 3
1. The entity assumption	0.2413	-0.0190	0.3497
2. The going concern assumption	0.2353	-0.5982	0.8683
3. The stable monetary unit assumption	0.0022	-1.4585	-1.3549
4. The period assumption	-0.1446	0.9082	1.8595
5. The cost principle	-0.7469	-0.5209	-0.7631
6. The revenue principle	0.3756	-0.7796	-1.2843
7. The matching principle	-0.9497	-1.6190	1.3517
8. The objectivity principle	-0.2063	-0.0455	0.1575
9. The consistency	2.2555	0.2260	-0.3862
10. The full disclosure principle	1.4267	1.4771	-0.3862
11. The materiality principle	-1.2672	1.1718	-0.7412
12. The conservation principle	-1.2220	1.2576	0.7518

pothesis is provided by the results in the sense that cultural affiliations lead to different cognitions or systems of knowledge, which in turn may lead to different approaches to the understanding of accounting relationships.

Intragroup Perceptual Differences

To determine whether the observed difference in cognitions or systems of knowledge held, after allowing for the subject's background, the subjects' salience for each of the three dimensions were regressed against the following variables: (1) the subject's age; (2) the number of years in the accounting firm; (3) the number of years in his/her present familiarity with financial statements. Exhibit 2.3 reports the results of the regressions analysis. The four independent variables have no effect on the subjects' cognitions as represented by three-dimensional space. Therefore, the accounting concept perception and the resulting salience could be considered as independent of these variables.

DISCUSSION

The results suggest that intercultural differences exist in the perception of accounting concepts on two of the three dimensions of a common perceptual space. The results imply that the meanings of accounting concepts do vary in the manner with which they can be recognized, grasped, or

Exhibit 2.2
Results of the Analysis of Variance on Three Dimensions' Salience

Source of Dimensions

variation	Conjunctive				Relational				Disjunctive			
	df	Sum of squares	Mean squares	F	df	Sum of squares	Mean squares	F	df	Sum of squares	Mean squares	F
Model	2	0.0047	0.0023	2.77**	2	0.0054	0.00270	2.61**	2	0.00011	0.00005	0.15
Error	84	0.0724	0.0008		84	0.0870	0.00103		84	0.03301		
Total	86	0.0772			86	0.0924			86	0.03303		

**Significant at alpha = 0.10

Exhibit 2.3
Regression Results on the Dimensions' Salience

Source of Dimensions

variation	Conjunctive				Relational				Disjunctive			
	df	Sum of squares	Mean squares	F	df	Sum of squares	Mean squares	F	df	Sum of squares	Mean squares	F
Model	4	0.0029	0.00073	0.78	4	0.00566	0.0014	1.28	4	0.0024	0.00061	0.59
Error	84	0.0739	0.00094		78	0.08645	0.0011		78	0.0302		
Total	82	0.0769			82	0.09212			82			

understood by users from different cultural groups. These intercultural differences agree with the cultural determinism thesis that various cultural affiliations in accounting create different cognitions or systems of knowledge, which in turn lead to a different understanding of accounting constructs.

This study has isolated the effects of culture on the perception of accounting concepts by controlling for (a) organizational culture (the subjects were all professional accountants), (b) occupational culture (the subjects were all professional accountants), (c) the managerial culture (the subjects were all partners or managers), and (d) linguistic relativism (the subjects were all anglophones). The results were indicative of communications problems that may arise in the perception of accounting concepts as a result of differences in the cognition or systems of knowledge of each particular culture.

The findings have general implications for the study and practice of accounting internationally. The general practice in international accounting has been for the observer to start with a set of assumed universal theoretical premises before attempting an inquiry across cultures. In doing so, an "etic" approach is adopted, taking the perspective of the observer as an important ingredient for the generation of scientifically predictive theories about the causes of sociocultural differences and similarities. Given the cultural relativism results found in this study, an "emic" approach is preferable as: (1) it studies behavior from within the system, (2) it examines one culture at a time, (3) it uses a structure discovered by the analyst (rather than created by the analyst), and (4) it uses criteria that are relative to the internal characteristics (rather than criteria that are assumed absolute or universal). The emic approach to cultural determinism to accounting, as advocated by this study's results, holds that culture determines and/or influences accounting techniques. An adoption of the emic approach to cultural relativism and cross-cultural research in accounting will allow the discipline to (1) establish the boundary conditions for accounting models and theories, (2) evaluate the impact of cultural and ecological factors in accounting contexts, and (3) identify the few cultunits that represent deviant cases.

CONCLUSION

A selected set of accounting concepts was subjected to analysis using multidimensional scaling techniques to evaluate the intercultural differences between three groups of partners and managers from the same Big Six accounting firms. Cultural relativism was used to justify the possible lack of consensus on the meaning of accounting concepts as a result of different cognitions or systems of knowledge in the three cultures. The INDSCAL model applied to the matrix of similarity judgments enabled the identification of three dimensions and subjects' salience. The dimensions were labeled as conjunctive, relational, or disjunctive by analogy to the process of concept formation. An analysis of variance applied to the individual salience verified the cultural determinism thesis for two of three dimensions of a common cognitive space. These results indicate basic communication problems in the perceptions of accounting concepts as a result of differences in the cognition or system of knowledge of each particular culture. It appears then that the subjects from different cultures differ in their perception of accounting concepts independently of the differences in age, number of years in the accounting firm, number of years in the present position, and the degree of familiarity with financial statements. These differences are basic differences arising from cultural differences in the perception of accounting concepts. These differences may be explained by differences in value systems, placing different emphasis on the meaning of each of the accounting concepts examined in this study. For example, differences in the perception of conservatism are consistent with the cultural differences on uncertainty avoidance. As stated by Gray: "A preference for more conservative measures of profits is consistent with strong uncertainty avoidance following from a concern with security and a perceived need to adopt a cautious approach to cope with uncertainty of future events." Therefore, the results observed in this study show that the differences in the perception of accounting concepts are reconcilable with differences in societal values that have a definite impact on accounting values. Given these communication problems, one may envision inconsistencies in audit behavior, financial analysis, accounting method choice, and so on. Further research is needed on these subjects, especially in terms of allowing for the investigation of the combined effects of culture as cognition on the one hand, and organizational culture, occupational culture, managerial culture, and linguistic relativism on the other. In short, these preliminary results point to the need for more conceptual and empirical research on the nature and consequences of cultural determinism in accounting. One area of interest would be the ethical conflicts confronting multinational accounting firms. This issue is addressed in Appendix 2.1.

NOTES

1. Geert Hofstede, "The Cultural Context of Accounting," in Barry E. Cushing, ed., *Accounting and Culture* (Sarasota, Fla.: American Accounting Association, 1987), pp. 1–11.

2. Hein Schreuder, "Accounting Research, Practice and Culture: A European Perspective," in Barry E. Cushing, ed., *Accounting and Culture* (Sarasota, Fla.: American Accounting Association, 1987), pp. 12–22.

3. William J. Violet, "The Development of International Accounting Standards: An Anthropological Perspective," *International Journal of Accounting Education and Research* (Spring 1983).

4. Geert Hofstede, "The Ritual Nature of Accounting Systems," paper presented at EIASM Workshop, "Accounting and Culture," Amsterdam, June 5–7, 1985.

5. J. Soeters and U. Schreuder, "The Interaction Between National and Organizational Cultures in Accounting Firms," *Accounting, Organizations and Society* 13, no. 1 (1988): 75–86.

6. Gilles Chavalier, "Should Accounting Practices Be Universal?" *Canadian Chartered Accountant Magazine* (July 1977): 47–50.

7. J. Acheson, "Accounting Concepts and Economic Opportunities in a Tarascan Village: Emic and Etic Views," *Human Organization* (Spring 1972): 83–91.

8. D. Alhashim, "Accounting Control Through Purposive Uniformity," *International Journal of Accounting Education and Research* (Spring 1973).

9. R.D. Nair and W.G. Frank, "The Impact of Disclosure and Measurement Practices on International Accounting Classification," *The Accounting Review* (July 1980).

10. Garnett F. Beazley, "An International Implication for Accounting," *International Journal of Accounting Education and Research* (Spring 1968).

11. D. McComb, "International Harmonization of Accounting: A Cultural Dimension," *International Journal of Accounting Education and Research* (Spring 1979).

12. M. Bromwich and A.G. Hopwood, eds., *Accounting Standard Setting: An International Perspective* (London: Pitman, 1983).

13. A. Belkaoui, "Economic, Political and Civil Indicators and Reporting and Disclosure Adequacy: Empirical Investigation," *Journal of Accounting and Public Policy* (Fall 1983).

14. A. Belkaoui, *International Accounting* (Westport, Conn.: Quorum Books, 1985.

15. M.H.B. Perera and M.R. Mathews, "The Interrelationship of Culture and Accounting with Particular Reference to Social Accounting," (discussion paper no. 59, Department of Accounting and Finance, Massey University, 1987).

16. Linda Smircich, "Concepts of Culture and Organizational Analysis," *Administrative Science Quarterly* 28 (September 1983): 339–58.

17. Bronislaw Malinowski, *A Scientific Theory of Culture* (Chapel Hill: The University of North Carolina Press, 1944).

18. A.R. Radcliffe-Brown, *Structure and Function in Primitive Society* (New York: Free Press, 1968).

19. Ward H. Goodenough, *Culture, Language and Society* (Reading, Mass.: Addison-Wesley, 1971).

20. Charles Frake, "The Ethnographic Study of Cognitive Systems," in Joshua A. Fishman, ed., *Reading in the Sociology of Language* (The Hague, Netherlands: Mouton, 1968), pp. 434–46.

21. Phillip K. Bock, *Continuities in Psychological Anthropology* (San Francisco: W.H. Freeman, 1980) pp. 227-46.

22. Clifford Geertz, *The Interpretation of Cultures* (New York: Basic Books, 1973).

23. Claude Levi-Strauss, *Structural Anthropology* (Chicago: University of Chicago Press, 1983).

24. Ino Rossi and Edurin O'Higgins, "The Development of Theories of Culture," in Ino Rossi, ed., *People in Culture* (New York: Praeger, 1980) pp. 31–78.

25. Ibid.

26. F.W. Young, "TORSCA–9: An IBM 360/7S FORTRAN IV Program for Nonmetric Multidimensional Scaling," *Journal of Marketing Research* (1968): 319–20.

27. A. Belkaoui, *Accounting Theory* (San Diego, Calif.: Harcourt Brace and Jovanovich, 1985).

28. J.B. Kruskal, "Multidimensional Scaling by Optimizing Goodness of Fit to a Nonmetric Hypothesis," *Psychometrica* 29 (1964): 1–27.

29. J.B. Kruskal, "Nonmetric Multidimensional: A Numerical Method," *Psychometrica* 29 (1964): 28–42.

30. Joan E. Miller, Roger N. Shepard, and Jih-Jih Chang, "An Analytical Approach to the Interpretation of Multidimensional Scaling Solutions," *American Psychologist* (September 1969): 579–80.

31. J.W. McDavid and H. Harari, *Psychology and Social Behavior* (New York: Harper and Row, 1974).

32. D.E. Hunt and C.I. Hovland, "Order of Consideration of Different Types of Concepts," *Journal of Experimental Psychology* (1960): 220–5.

33. David Klahr, "A Monte Carlo Investigation of the Statistical Significance of Kruskal's Nonmetric Scaling Procedure," *Psychometrica* (September 1969): 319–30.

REFERENCES

Acheson, J. "Accounting Concepts and Economic Opportunities in a Tarascan Village: Emic and Etic Views." *Human Organization* (Spring 1972): 83–91.

Alhashim, D. "Accounting Control Through Purposive Uniformity." *International Journal of Accounting Education and Research* (Spring 1973).

Argyris, Chris, and Donald Schon. *Organizational Learning.* Reading, Mass.: Addison-Wesley, 1978.

Beazley, Garnett F. "An International Implication for Accounting." *International Journal of Accounting Education and Research* (Spring 1968).

Belkaoui, A. *Accounting Theory.* San Diego, Calif.: Harcourt Brace and Jovanovich, 1985.

———. *International Accounting.* Westport, Conn: Quorum Books, 1985.

———. "Economic, Political and Civil Indicators and Reporting and Disclosure Adequacy: Empirical Investigation." *Journal of Accounting and Public Policy* (Fall 1983).

———. "The Interprofessional Linguistic Communication of Accounting Concepts: An Experiment in Sociolinguistics." *Journal of Accounting Research* (Autumn 1980): 362-74.

———. "Linguistic Relativity in Accounting." *Accounting, Organizations and Society* 2 (1978): 97–104.

Bock, Phillip K. *Continuities in Psychological Anthropology.* San Francisco: W.H. Freeman, 1980, pp. 227-46.

Bougon, Michel. "Uncovering Cognitive Maps: The Self-Q Technique." In *Beyond*

Method: Social Research Strategies, edited by Careth Morgan. Beverly Hills, Calif.: Sage, 1983.

Bougon, Michel, Karl Weich, and Buikhost Din. "Cognition in Organizations: An Analysis of the Utrecht Jazy Orchestra." *Administrative Science Quarterly* 22 (1977): 606–39.

Bromwich, M., and A.G. Hopwood, eds. *Accounting Standard Setting: An International Perspective*. London: Pitman, 1983.

Caroll, J.D., and J.J. Chang. "Analysis of Individual Differences in Multidimensional Scaling Via N-Way Generalization of 'Eckart-Young' Decomposition." *Psychometrika* 35 (1970): 238–319.

Chevalier, Gilles. "Should Accounting Practices Be Universal?" *The Canadian Chartered Accountant Magazine* (July 1977): 47–50.

Choi, F.D.S., and G.G. Mueller. *International Accounting*. Englewood Cliffs, N.J.: Prentice-Hall, 1984.

Flamholtz, E., and E. Cook. "Cognitive Meaning and Its Role in Accounting Change: A Field Study." *Accounting, Organizations and Society* (October 1978).

Frake, Charles. "The Ethnographic Study of Cognitive Systems." In *Reading in the Sociology of Language*, edited by Joshua A. Fishman. The Hague, Netherlands: Mouton, 1968, pp. 434-46.

Geertz, Clifford. *The Interpretation of Cultures*. New York: Basic Books, 1973.

Goodenough, Ward H. *Culture, Language and Society*. Reading, Mass.: Addison-Wesley, 1971.

Grant, D.A. "Perceptual Versus Analytical Responses to the Number Concept of a Weigel-type Card Sorting Test." *Journal of Experimental Psychology* (1951): 23–29.

Gray, S.J. "Towards a Theory of Cultural Influence on the Development of Accounting Systems Internationally." *Abacus* (March 1988): 1–15.

Harris, Linda, and Vernon Cronen. "A Rules Based Model for the Analysis and Evaluation of Organizational Communications." *Communications Quarterly* (Winter 1979): 12–28.

Heidbreder, E., M. Bensley, and M. Ivy. "The Attainment of Concepts: IV. Regularities and Levels." *Journals of Psychology* (1960): 220–25.

Hofstede, Geert. "The Cultural Context of Accounting." In *Accounting and Culture*, edited by Barry E. Cushing. Sarasota, Fla.: American Accounting Association, 1987, pp. 1-11.

———. "The Ritual Nature of Accounting Systems." Paper presented at EIASM Workshop, "Accounting and Culture," Amsterdam, June 5–7, 1985.

Hunt, D.E., and C.I. Hovland. "Order of Consideration of Different Types of Concepts." *Journal of Experimental Psychology* (1960): 220–25.

Klahr, David. "A Monte Carlo Investigation of the Statistical Significance of Kruskal's Nonmetric Scaling Procedure." *Psychometrica* (September 1969): 319–30.

Kruskal, J.B. "Multidimensional Scaling by Optimizing Goodness of Fit to a Nonmetric Hypothesis." *Psychometrica* 29 (1964): 1–27.

———. "Nonmetric Multidimensional: A Numerical Method." *Psychometrica* 29 (1964): 28–42.

Levi-Strauss, Claude. *Structural Anthropology*. Chicago: University of Chicago Press, 1983.

Litterer, Joseph A., and Stanley Young. "The Development of Managerial Reflective Skills." Proceedings, Northeast AIDS (April 1981).

McComb, D. "International Harmonization of Accounting: A Cultural Dimension." *International Journal of Accounting Education and Research* (Spring 1979).

McDavid, J.W., and H. Harari. *Psychology and Social Behavior*. New York: Harper and Row, 1974.

Malinowski, B. *A Scientific Theory of Culture*. Chapel Hill: The University of North Carolina Press, 1944.

Miller, Joan E., Roger N. Shepard, and Jih-Jih Chang. "An Analytical Approach to the Interpretation of Multidimensional Scaling Solutions." *American Psychologist* (September 1969): 579–80.

Monti-Belkaoui, J., and Ahmed Belkaoui. "Bilingualism and the Perception of Professional Concepts." *Journal of Psycholinguistic Research* 2 (1983): 111–27.

Mueller, Gerhard G. *International Accounting*. New York: MacMillan, 1967.

Nair, R.D., and W.G. Frank. "The Impact of Disclosure and Measurement Practices on International Accounting Classification." *The Accounting Review* (July 1980).

Nobes, C.W. *International Classification of Financial Reporting*. London: Croom Helm, 1984.

————. "A Judgmental International Classification of Financial Reporting Practices." *Journal of Business Finance and Accounting* (Spring 1983).

Perera, M.H.B., and M.R. Mathews. "The Interrelationship of Culture and Accounting with Particular Reference to Social Accounting." Discussion paper no. 59, Department of Accounting and Finance, Massey University, 1987.

Radcliffe-Brown, A.R. *Structure and Function in Primitive Society*. New York: Free Press, 1968.

Rossi, Ino, and Edurin O'Higgins. "The Development of Theories of Culture." In *People in Culture*, edited by Ino Rossi. New York: Praeger, 1980, pp. 31–78.

Schreuder, Hein. "Accounting Research, Practice and Culture: A European Perspective." In *Accounting and Culture*, edited by Barry E. Cushing. Sarasota, Fla.: American Accounting Association, 1987, pp. 12–22.

Singhvi, S. Surendra. "Characteristics and Implications of Inadequate Disclosure: A Case Study of India." *International Journal of Accounting Education and Research* (Spring 1978).

Smircich, Linda. "Concepts of Culture and Organizational Analysis." *Administrative Science Quarterly* (September 1983): 339–58.

Soeters, J., and U. Schreuder. "The Interaction Between National and Organizational Cultures in Accounting Firms." *Accounting, Organizations and Society* 13, no. 1 (1988): 75–86.

Violet, William J. "The Development of International Accounting Standards: An Anthropological Perspective." *International Journal of Accounting Education and Research* (Spring 1983).

Wacker, Gerald. "Toward a Cognitive Methodology of Organizational Assessment." *Journal of Applied Behavioral Science* 17 (1981): 114–29.

Weick, Karl E. "Cognitive Processes in Organizations." In *Research in Organizational Behavior*, edited by Larry L. Cummings and Barry M. Staw. (Greenwich, Conn.: JAI Press, 1979), pp. 41–74.

———. *The Social Psychology of Organizations*. Reading Mass.: Addison-Wesley, 1979.

Young, F.W. "TORSCA–9: An IBM 360/7S FORTRAN IV Program for Nonmetric Multidimensional Scaling." *Journal of Marketing Research* (1968): 319–20.

APPENDIX 2.1
QUESTIONNAIRE

1. Name:_____

2. Age:_____

3. Area of Undergraduate Studies:_____

4. Number of Accounting Courses Taken:_____

5.

Based on your background and experience, indicate the degree of importance you would assign to each piece of the following information when comparing the financial performance of two firms.

Circle the number corresponding to your evaluation.

	NOT IMPORTANT					EXTREMELY IMPORTANT	
Balance Sheet	1	2	3	4	5	6	7
Profit and Loss Statement	1	2	3	4	5	6	7
Funds Flow Statement	1	2	3	4	5	6	7

6. Consider the Following Accounting Hypotheses

   Hypothesis No. 1 Entity Assumption

             No. 2 Going Concern Assumption

             No. 3 Stable Monetary Unit Assumption

             No. 4 Period Assumption

             No. 5 Cost Principle

             No. 6 Revenue Priniple

APPENDIX 2.1 (continued)

No. 7   Matching Principle

No. 8   Objectivity Principle

No. 9   Consistency Principle

No.10   Full Disclosure Principle

No.11   Materiality Principle

No.12   Conservatism Principle

Assuming you are familiar with these accounting hypotheses, indicate the degree of similarity of each pair of concepts. The criteria to be used are left to your discretion - be consistent in your evaluation.

Example: If you think that hypotheses 1 and 2 are very dissimilar accounting concepts, circle 1.

Hypothesis 1 & Hypothesis 2

Very   Very

Dissimilar   1   2   3   4   5   6   7   Similar

Hypothesis 1 & Hypothesis 3

Very   Very

Dissimilar   1   2   3   4   5   6   7   Similar

Hypothesis 1 & Hypothesis 4

Very   Very

APPENDIX 2.1 (continued)

Dissimilar   1   2   3   4   5   6   7   Similar

Hypothesis 10 & Hypothesis 11

Very   Very

Dissimilar   1   2   3   4   5   6   7   Similar

Hypothesis 10 & Hypothesis 12

Very   Very

Dissimilar   1   2   3   4   5   6   7   Similar

Hypothesis 11 & Hypothesis 1

Very   Very

Dissimilar   1   2   3   4   5   6   7   Similar

Hypothesis 11 & Hypothesis 12

Very   Very

Dissimilar   1   2   3   4   5   6   7   Similar

7. List the criteria used for assigning similarities in question no. 3.

· _____

·_____

· _____

· _____

· _____

APPENDIX 2.1 (continued)

8. Please provide the following background information.

    1. What year were you born? 19__ .

    2. To the nearest year, how many years have you been employed in this firm?

    3. To the nearest year, how many years have you been employed in the present position?

        _____ years.

    4. Describe the exact nature of the activities of your department or group. Be specific.

        _____

        _____

        _____

    5. The results of this research will be mailed to you if you indicate your name and address:

        _____

        _____

        _____

9. Thank you very much for your cooperation and support.

APPENDIX 2.2
CULTURE-BASED ETHICAL CONFLICTS CONFRONTING MULTINATIONAL ACCOUNTING FIRMS

SYNOPSIS: The mergers and the international expansion of the Big Six firms have created a new class of problems for their management. Local partners must not only continue to meet the diverse needs of local clients with improved service levels in response to the higher level of competition; they must now, in common with managers of other multinational businesses, also address the problem of global coordination. This is not just a matter of providing a seamless, high quality international audit service to their global clients. It includes the worldwide management of the standardization of activities such as the audit process, hiring and promotion criteria, and implementation of the firm's code of professional conduct at the local level in a wide diversity of cultures.

This paper uses Hofstede's (1980, 1991) measures of national culture to provide a framework for identifying ethical problems arising from cultural differences in international audit practice. A wealth of anecdotal evidence supports the view that auditors in different countries have different ethical perceptions and standards. For example, McKinnon (1984) describes the conflict experienced by Japanese external auditors who had to pressure clients for access to financial information previously considered private. To help ensure optimal audit quality as well as the highest possible ethical behavior, multinational accounting firms need to manage a diversity of standards and practices.[1] The purpose of this paper is to integrate cross-cultural issues and ethics by using Hofstede's (1980, 1991) widely accepted measures of cultural differences (Harrison 1992; Frucot and Shearon 1991; and Lee and Green 1991) to identify cross-national problems in auditor ethical decision-making. The focus of this paper is to highlight the cultural factors that influence auditors' ethical perspectives regarding questionable client behavior. A systematic knowledge of the differences in professionals' ethical sensitivities and the way ethical choices are made would be invaluable for formulating guidelines for a firm-wide ethical policy. It also could provide international firms with a framework with which to identify potential ethical problem-areas in specific countries.

We first briefly examine the possible influence of international cultural factors on ethical perceptions and then review professional ethics in the international accounting profession. Next we explore the relationship between Hofstede's (1980, 1991) measures of culture, and ethical issues pertinent to auditing. We present examples of culture-based ethical conflicts and consider their implications for effective control of ethical behavior in international auditing firms. The paper concludes with suggestions for enhancing effective control systems in international auditing firms.

---

[1]For example, Purvis et al. (1991) describe the difficulties encountered by the International Accounting Standards Committee (IASC) project to develop comparability of financial standards across countries.

We gratefully acknowledge the helpful comments of Theresa Hammond, Gil Manzon, anonymous reviewers and several current and former members of multinational accounting firms who asked to remain anonymous. This manuscript was the recipient of the 1992 best international accounting paper award sponsored by the Association of Chartered Accountants in the United States.

From Jeffrey R. Cohen, Laurie W. Pant, and David J. Sharp, "Culture-Based Ethical Conflicts Confronting Multinational Accounting Firms," *Accounting Horizons* (September 1993): 1–13. Reprinted with Permission.

CROSS-CULTURAL DIFFERENCES IN ETHICAL PERCEPTIONS

Several researchers have found cross-national differences in ethical reasoning in a business context. Becker and Fritsche (1987) in a mail survey of managers from France, Germany and the United States compared attitudes towards corporate codes of ethical conduct and towards a series of statements concerning the ethics of current business practices. Some of the more interesting inter-country differences were that the French had more faith that a formal code of ethics would ensure ethical behavior than did the American and German samples, and that the German sample was most likely to believe that the spiritual and moral consequences of a decision were not the concern of a business person. Dubinsky et al. (1991) investigated the differences in ethical perceptions among American, Japanese and South Korean industrial sales people. Using a unidimensional ethical perception measure, they found significant differences among the three groups, and suggested that they might be attributable to national differences in work environments, which in turn might reflect cultural differences. For example, the U.S. salespeople in general found the scenarios to contain less ethical conflict than the Japanese or Koreans. The U.S. subjects also felt a greater need for explicit written policies to address ethical dilemmas.

Langlois and Schlegelmilch (1990) compared the content of American and European (French, British, and West German) corporate codes of conduct. Treating "Europe" as a single culture, they found that European companies stress the right of codetermination and a sense of belonging and responsibility (familial-type relationships) while American codes stress fairness and equity. Tsalikis and Nwachukwu (1991) compared Nigerian and American business students' views on bribery and extortion and also found significant cross-national differences. They also investigated within-country differences and found that respondents' perceptions of the immorality of an action was a function of the nationality of the actor rela-

tive to the nationality of the respondent. For example, the Nigerian sample viewed as more unethical a bribe given and/or received by a foreigner than one given and/or received by a local national. Thus, a review of the cross-cultural literature suggests that there are international differences in perceptions of what constitutes ethical. We will now turn to how ethics has been addressed in the international accounting domain.

INTERNATIONAL ACCOUNTING ETHICS

The restructuring of the profession has led to increased competitive pressures in both the United States and abroad, promoting responses such as aggressive pricing strategies (e.g., lowballing) and diversification into nontraditional areas such as consulting, which raise the possibility of threatened auditor independence (Warren and Wilkerson 1988; Auditing Practices Board 1992). These changes present multinational firms with new and unfamiliar ethical dilemmas within a variety of local auditing and financial reporting standards.[2] The International Federation of Accountants (IFAC) has recognized the need to confront ethical issues among accountants by adopting a proactive approach to ethics with its promulgation of the "Guideline on Ethics for Professional Accountants" (1990) and the Exposure Draft on "Professional Ethics for Accountants: The Educational Challenge and Practical Application" (1992). The following excerpt from IFAC's proposed guideline on education speaks to the profession's recognition of the centrality of ethics to accounting:

---

[2]It is true that many public accounting firms have been operating internationally for years and have established audit procedures. For example, in conversation with one author, a partner in one Big Six firm stated that firm-wide audit policies were developed by an internal international committee. Some of the initial positions on audit requirements that were derived for their U.S. practice have been relaxed to become more general where those rules are in conflict with or unnecessarily restrictive in comparison to local requirements. The responsibility for implementation and review of these procedures lies with U.S. management — the group perceived to follow the strictest requirements for attestation.

Professional accountants today have an increasing role in decision making. This applies whether they are working in public practice, in industry or commerce, in the public sector or in education. They operate in a world of change in which corporate collapse, business impropriety, regulatory failure and environmental disaster are prevalent.

In such an environment, accountants need to have a thorough appreciation of the potential implications of professional and management decisions and an awareness of the pressures of observing and upholding ethical standards which may fall on individuals involved in the decision making process. (IFAC 1992, 1-2)

Both the IFAC guidelines on ethics and its exposure draft on education recognize the diversity of worldwide practice and are designed to help auditors play a critical role in reducing fraudulent financial reporting. IFAC's guideline on education recognizes that solutions to the educational challenge will be reached locally, and therefore, differentially implemented. However, the guidelines make no explicit recognition of the worldwide diversity of cultures and ethical views and standards, but begins immediately to discuss the need to bring firms' professionals up to speed regarding ethical issues. We note that the firms' top management and the profession's standard setters are unlikely to be fully sensitive to international and cultural differences. Given the recent rapid internationalization of firms, management of these auditing firms need more information on the nature and extent of international ethical diversity in order to adequately control for such differences. Varying socioeconomic and cultural factors within an international auditing context (Cohen et al. 1992), have made the control of an international auditing firm more complex. Hofstede's measures of national culture provide a useful structure for understanding these complex issues.

HOFSTEDE'S MEASURES OF NATIONAL CULTURE

Hofstede (1980) defined culture as the collective mental programming that distinguishes one group from another. The program-

ming manifests itself in the values and beliefs of a society. Values are the tendency of an individual to prefer certain states of affairs over others. For any number of social behaviors, societies put different weights on different outcomes. Often these factors require a "guns or butter" tradeoff, and elements in the society are strongly anchored to preferences for one outcome over the other. Hofstede argues that the level at which preferences find their equilibrium is culturally determined. In his study of 116,000 IBM employees from over 50 nations conducted over several years, Hofstede identified four work-related values that differed systematically across cultures. He labeled these Uncertainty Avoidance, Individualism-Collectivism, Masculinity-Femininity, and Power Distance. These cultural dimensions have proven useful in cross-cultural studies in accounting (Harrison 1992; Frucot and Shearon 1991; Soeters and Schreuder 1988). Subsequent research reported by Hofstede and Bond (1988) identified a fifth cultural dimension, Short Term/Long Term orientation. We will first explain each of the five dimensions and, in turn, discuss how they affect the effective implementation of an auditing firm's worldwide codes of ethical conduct.

UNCERTAINTY AVOIDANCE

Uncertainty avoidance measures the way cultures face an unknown future with differing anxiety levels, need for security, and dependence upon experts. Hofstede describes an individual's high intolerance of ambiguity by "tendencies toward rigidity and dogmatism, intolerance of different opinions, traditionalism, superstition, racism, and ethnocentrism" (Hofstede 1980, 155). Society's response to ambiguity is exhibited by attempts to reduce the level of the unknown through extending the domains of technology, law, and religion. In work-related situations, the need for predictability, rules, and job stability indicates strong uncertainty avoidance.

Hofstede argues that the response of organizations and individuals is less related to an absolute or objective level of uncertainty in a situation than to perceptions about the level of uncertainty. For organizations, the environment is perceived as the source of uncertainties. A firm's response to these uncertainties is operationalized through technology, rules and rituals. Technology attempts to create known patterns of activities in physical processes. Rules and regulations try to make an individual's behavior predictable and in accordance with a set of values. Rituals (e.g., management development programs or the omnipresent business meetings) support social cohesion, can serve as initiation rites and support the values of the participants. Hofstede includes within the category of rituals such organizational activities as the organization's planning and control systems, variance analysis, memo writing, and the use of respected outside experts.

ETHICAL IMPLICATIONS OF UNCERTAINTY AVOIDANCE

Hofstede's measure of uncertainty avoidance (UA) includes three elements: rule orientation, employment stability, and stress. For the accounting profession, rules are of the upmost importance. Cushing and Loebbecke (1986) found that large accounting firms' audit methodologies differed along a "structured-unstructured" dimension. For example, highly structured firms provide extensive rules and guidelines for materiality judgments (consistent with strong uncertainty avoidance) while unstructured firms provide much fewer guidelines.

Hofstede examined whether members of different cultures believed that company rules should be broken — even when doing so would be in the company's best interests. This captures an individual's willingness to tolerate the ambiguity of outcomes when going beyond the rules, and is related to at least two auditing issues. The first is the form versus content debate over whether an auditing rule should be followed literally, or whether the underlying intent of the rule should be interpreted and implemented when the intent is at odds with the existing operationalization of the rule. In the US auditing environment,

this conflict has been raised in regard to the auditor's role in the S&L crisis. A second issue surrounds any apparent conflict of interest situation. Questions about providing or receiving other services beyond the audit (e.g., providing MAS services, accepting home mortgage loans from an S&L audit client) are thought to be at the boundaries of conflict of interest. Disagreement with a rule-orientation approach would indicate a higher tolerance for ambiguity — it is acceptable, even appropriate, to break company rules on occasion if doing so is in the company's and/or society's best interest. Interestingly, in strong uncertainty avoidance cultures Hofstede argues that rules can bestow an aura of "truth" which excludes the possibility of other truths.

In the international auditing environment, the uncertainty avoidance construct has particularly interesting implications for ethical decision making. The profession's focus is on objective reporting of financial results. The rapid innovation of complex business and financial transactions has developed faster than accounting rule-makers have been able to respond to them (e.g., software development, cross-border financing contracts). This lag results in inadequate or nonexistent accounting rules leading to an even greater dependence on auditor judgment. Auditors from cultures with a higher tolerance for ambiguity (including Denmark, Great Britain, the US, and Sweden with weak uncertainty avoidance scores) should be more likely than auditors from cultures having strong UA scores (e.g., Greece, Portugal, Japan) to focus on the content of the issue rather than on the form alone. In contrast, countries with strong uncertainty avoidance have an "[e]motional need for rules, even if these will never work" and have a high "resistance to innovation" (Hofstede 1991, 125). For example, in complicated issues over mergers or joint ventures, auditors from strong UA cultures such as in Latin and South America are more likely to be satisfied by following existing rules. But, more importantly, this use of a "black and white" lens approach that defines what is unacceptable as only that which has been explicitly prohibited is an issue for concern. In these cultures, the absence of existing rules may make complying with a client's aggressive approach to financial reporting more acceptable for auditors.

To illustrate this, consider the case of a US auditor of a US manufacturer whose Italian agent earns a $200,000 commission for making a sale in Italy.[3] Suppose that the principal of the agency is a 100 percent owner and asks that the commission be paid to a personal Swiss bank account. It might be suspected that the purpose of the payment arrangement is to avoid paying Italian income taxes. The owner is probably neither paying the incurred taxes nor properly reporting the marketing firm's financial results, both illegal in Italy. Often the laws of neither the client's nor the auditor's country specifically address how they should react to the conflict. It is highly likely that members of a strong UA culture would interpret the absence of a rule forbidding this transaction as a license to accept it. In general, auditors from strong UA cultures are more likely to equate "legal" with "ethical" responsibilities. In contrast, when specific legal sanctions are missing, those in low UA cultures might apply a broader ethical framework to decisions and refrain from questionable actions even if they were legal.

A similar case can be made for areas of apparent conflict of interest for auditors. When no precise rule regarding a specific behavior exists, the auditor from a strong UA culture may find it easier to accept the client's behavior. Third-world software piracy provides an interesting illustration. Consider a local audit client who pirates a product and then uses it in a production process. An auditor from a strong UA culture will look for rules — in this case, the Berne Convention, an international agreement on copyrights under which copying is illegal. However, in countries that have not signed the Berne Convention, piracy is not necessarily illegal. If the auditor of this firm also audits the software firm whose product was copied, what is the auditor's responsibility? This problem already exists for auditors of some Pacific Rim manufacturers. For example, close imitations ("knockoffs") of toys, clothes, and electronics are not always prohibited by local law. An au-

dit firm could find itself being engaged by two clients, the creator of the product and an Asian imitator. Local auditors in strong UA countries would likely have few qualms about working for and advising both firms. In contrast, auditors from weak UA cultures would probably experience a conflict of interest in maintaining both clients or in remaining with the imitator client.

INDIVIDUALISM

Individualism describes the way an individual relates to and lives within his/her society. A good example illustrating differences in individualism is the nature of the family unit. Individualist societies such as those in the US and Europe live in nuclear families, while collectivist societies in many African or Asian countries live around extended families, clans, or tribal units. This relationship of the individual to the group results in behaviors and values which in turn affect the society's other institutions including education, religion, and politics. The central value is captured by how the individual thinks of him/herself as an individual relative to the group. Hofstede uses the illustration of religious conversion to capture this individualist/collectivist dimension. In western societies, the choice to change religions is totally personal. However, in more collectivist cultures, conversion is a step taken by a family or a tribe. In general, Hofstede found that wealthier countries tend to be individualist while poorer countries tend to be collectivist in orientation.

ETHICAL IMPLICATIONS OF INDIVIDUALISM

Of all five constructs, individualism is the most highly associated with moral values in American society (deTocqueville 1956). Hofstede (1991, 58) notes that in individualist cultures, speaking one's mind is a virtue, and confrontation to achieve a higher truth is a praiseworthy goal. In contrast, in collectivist societies, it is considered rude and unde-

[3]This example and aspects of several others described here were suggested in a conversation with one international audit partner of a Big Six firm.

sirable to confront another individual. Anglo-American countries are especially individualistic (in fact five of the six most individualistic of the over 50 countries in Hofstede's study are the US, Australia, Great Britain, Canada, and New Zealand). The Anglo-American perspective on auditing is a good illustration of individualism. Independence, that is, freedom from the influence of others, is a cornerstone of the Anglo-American audit. For example, maintaining freedom from the potential conflict of interest associated with being paid by the client is among the first topics of every basic Anglo-American auditing course. The implication is that all clients should be treated in the same fashion with no favoritism being shown. In contrast, in a collectivist society, preferential treatment is always extended to the ingroup, thus apparently imperiling the Anglo-American notion of independence.

In an organization, individualism is exhibited in the degree of dependence of members on their organization, and, in turn, the level of the organization's responsibility for its members. For multinational audit firms, this leads to an interesting conflict in collectivist countries. The scores of the US and Canada on the individualist-collectivist dimension are at the individualist end, while Japan lies towards the collectivist end. The "up or out" policy prevalent in most US and Canadian public accounting offices can cause conflicts with the expectations of employment longevity in collectivist societies such as in Japan. In addition, collectivist cultures like Japan place a high value on conformity to group norms. A Japanese individual would be much more likely than an American or Canadian to understate the importance of his or her own efforts in order to promote group harmony. This difference in cultural values has consequences for ethical behavior. For example, pressure on a subordinate to cover up a supervisor's illegal action such as accepting bribes might be evaluated differently by Japanese than Americans or Canadians because of cultural influences. While North Americans may interpret this pressure as coercion, Japanese may participate more willingly in a cover-up for communitarian motives - to protect the reputation of their group. This behavior was evident in recent (1991-1992) financial services scandals that included the largest investment banking firms in Japan.

As noted earlier, the Individualist/Collectivist dimension is particularly important in regard to the notion of independence. In the Anglo-American tradition, auditors are expected to ask tough questions of management and to report to them when the review of the organization indicates control weaknesses. The strong independence-based focus of North American audit tradition is exemplified by auditing's adherence to principles and society's expectation that its interests are protected only when the auditor blows the whistle — at least to management, or to the next auditor when there is a resignation from the audit. However, auditors from collectivist countries may react negatively to being told they have to request a representation letter from management.[4] Implicitly questioning management's integrity by asking the client to assure the auditor that the company's financial records are kept accurately and that an effective internal control is in place may be difficult within the auditor-client relationship in collectivist cultures. Further, the international auditor from a collectivist culture may find it both insulting and presumptuous to report to the audit committee on weaknesses in the client's internal control system. This is very private for the firm and not the responsibility of an outsider to embarrass management with such information. In contrast, the Anglo-American auditing tradition would look at an excessively close relationship between the auditor and management as totally contrary to protecting society's interests. This perspective would contradict the collectivist approach which is focused to protect the group from the outsider, even at the expense of the needs of the individual. In fact, Hofstede (1991, 62) argues that not treating an ingroup member better than someone from an outgroup would

---

[4]This example was suggested by a former manager in a Big Six international accounting firm.

be considered immoral in collectivist societies.[5]

MASCULINITY

The predominant socialization pattern of sex roles for most societies is for men to be more aggressive and for women to be more nurturing. Men, it is argued, translate this distinction into a need for achievement exhibited in winning, advancement, and higher earnings. Managers are expected to be decisive and if conflicts arise, they resolve them by fighting it out. In contrast, women's interests lie in relationships, rendering service, and attention to the environment. Moreover, female managers stress building consensus and resolving conflicts by compromise and negotiation. The ranking of a culture as more or less masculine is a function of the degree to which both sexes tend to prefer the more masculine goals. Out of 50 countries, Hofstede (1991) found Japan to be the most masculine while Sweden was the least masculine (the US was ranked 15th, Canada 24th, Great Britain 9th, Australia 16th).

ETHICAL IMPLICATIONS OF MASCULINITY

Because masculine-style behavior is usually more aggressive, there are important implications of the masculinity dimension for international ethical issues in the auditing profession. Hofstede argues that the mapping of the organization's goals (to get ahead, to make money) over the male manager's goals suggests that poor managers are those that are caring or non-aggressive. This translates into an implicit bias in performance evaluation against female managers. This bias is exacerbated internationally by an even greater emphasis on gender differentiated jobs. Hofstede's findings indicate that in more masculine countries, the values held by men and women in the same occupation tended to be different from the corresponding groups in the less masculine countries. Both the public accounting firm and the male auditors' goals and behavior are likely to be more aggressive, while the female auditors are likely to have

goals and behaviors based on different values that emphasize more cooperative non-confrontational behavior.

Gilligan (1982) posits that gender differences may affect ethical perceptions. Rosner (1990) discusses how women professionals differ from their male counterparts because they encourage participation, sharing power and information, and enhancing other people's self-worth. Betz et al. (1989) argue that gender socialization implies that women stress doing tasks well, promote harmonious relationships, and put less emphasis on competition among their colleagues. In a study of graduate business students, Betz et al. found that men were more likely than women to be interested in money, power, and rank in an organization, and that this gender socialization resulted in different evaluations of unethical behavior. Similar results were found by Whipple and Swords (1992) in a comparison of US and UK management students. Harris (1990) in a study of professionals in one service organization also found that women are significantly less tolerant of unethical behavior that promotes their self-interest than men are. Cohn (1991) noted that problems confronting upwardly mobile women accountants in Australia include a lack of access to networking, the notion that grey-haired women accountants will not be respected, and that men and women view success differently. This literature suggests that women will be less likely than men to be assertive and to "toot their own horn." As a result of the differences in gender socialization, local public accounting firm partners might be reluctant to hire, evaluate positively, and promote women in their offices. These gender differences have ethical implications for the accounting firm's control sys-

---

[5]However, for collectivist societies, the very familial nature of the group has its own correcting mechanisms. The family serves not only to protect individuals, but also to discipline them. Aberrant behavior is modified by pressure from the other group members through the notion of "shame" which invokes the ingroup's sense of honor. Perhaps a future study could examine the relative effectiveness of an audit conducted in a collectivist culture in which independence is apparently compromised from an Anglo-American perspective.

tem. Should the firm impose gender equality in local offices of high masculinity countries? Further, do high masculinity country gender biases create barriers against women looking for international assignments to strengthen their promotion potential?

POWER DISTANCE

Power distance describes the extent to which a society deals with human inequality in physical and mental characteristics, fame, wealth, power, and laws. Hofstede argues that people exhibit a pattern of dominance in the social order across cultures. However, the responses of cultures range from fairly formal systems of dominance in high power-distance cultures to elaborate attempts to de-emphasize dominance.

Within organizations, differences or inequality of ability and of power are accepted as functional. Hierarchies are the vehicle for assigning responsibilities and evaluation of the performance of those responsibilities. Hofstede argues that the boss-subordinate relationship is a function of objective realities (each party's expertise, the history of the relationship, and the nature and importance of the task at hand) and the culture's equilibrium between the subordinate's effort to reduce the inequality, and the boss' efforts to maintain or enlarge it. Hofstede defines power distance as "a measure of the interpersonal power of influence between B (boss) and S (subordinate) as perceived by the less powerful of the two" (1980, 98). For example, one of the questions included in this scale was "How frequently, in your experience, does the following problem occur: employees being afraid to express disagreement with their managers?" (1991, 25). The implication for such accepted tenets of US organizational control as participatory budgeting is quite evident. An attempt by a multinational public accounting firm to impose participatory budgeting in a high power distance country is likely to fail.

ETHICAL IMPLICATIONS OF POWER DISTANCE

One ethical aspect of this cultural dimension relates to the acceptability of a subordinate's obedience to a superior when told to perform unethical procedures. The US scores fairly low on Power Distance, and most western European countries (with the exception of France, Portugal and Spain) are also in the bottom half of Hofstede's Power Distance ranking. This unwillingness to accept large inequality of power is consistent with the need for auditors to exhibit high ethical standards even in the face of pressure from a superior. The attest function is predicated on the notion that auditors are not intimidated by large, wealthy clients, and can be independent from the client who pays them. The auditor must be able to insist when necessary on specific accounting treatments. In contrast, in high power distance countries (e.g., many Asian and African countries), a local auditor may have more difficulty resisting pressures from powerful and wealthy clients. As Hofstede wrote of High Power Distance countries, "Scandals involving persons in power are expected, and so is the fact that they will be covered up. If something goes wrong, the blame goes to people lower down the hierarchy" (1991, 38).

Hofstede found a strong correlation between high power distance and collectivism especially in Latin and Asian countries. (Hofstede argues that the dimensions are distinct when economic development is controlled for. Richer countries may exhibit strong individualism but moderate to weak power distance.) When higher power distance and collectivist characteristics describe the culture, subordinates will be likely to bend to the demands of their superiors .

The organizational structure of most accounting firms is pyramid-shaped, a power distance-enhancing format. Auditors are subject to pressure from their superiors. One common pressure is the need to complete an audit within budget and perhaps underreport the actual hours for an audit (Ponemon 1992). To the extent that this also creates incentives to curtail some audit procedures when judgment is necessary, a clear ethical problem exists. In countries where power distance is high, the subordinate is even more likely to feel compelled to acquiesce to a superior's request to either underreport or underperform the extent of audit work.

SHORT-TERM/LONG-TERM ORIENTATION (CONFUCIAN DYNAMISM)

A fifth cultural dimension emerged from a replication of Hofstede's (1980) study conducted with the view to eliminate its Western bias. Michael Bond, a colleague of Hofstede's, used Chinese social scientists from Hong Kong and Taiwan to develop a Chinese value survey (Hofstede and Bond 1988). Using 100 students (50 male and 50 female) in each of 22 countries, three of the dimensions described earlier also emerged from this survey. Uncertainty avoidance did not. Hofstede equates uncertainty avoidance with a search for truth and conjectures that for some societies, this search is not relevant. In its place, Bond's study revealed another dimension, a long-term versus a short-term orientation to life. The long-term perspective was reflected by a willingness to subordinate oneself for a group, ordering and observing relationships by status, thrift, perseverance towards slow results, and having a sense of shame. The short-term orientation exhibits social pressure to "keep up with the Joneses," protecting one's "face," respect for social and status obligations, reciprocation of greetings, favors, and gifts, and an expectation for quick results. Bond describes this dimension as Confucian because most of the values on both ends of the scale reflect the teachings of Confucius.

Organizationally, this dimension provides insight into the current concern over problems of US competitiveness related to a short-term focus of management and financial markets. Hofstede and Bond even suggest that it is no coincidence that the "Five Dragons" (Hong Kong, Taiwan, Japan, South Korea, and Singapore) score in the top nine countries having a long-term orientation (with Thailand — the country that has led the world in GNP growth during 1988 to 1990 — as another). They argue that the confluence of this long-term orientation with the correct economic and political conditions makes the economic miracle in these countries very understandable.

ETHICAL IMPLICATIONS OF LONG-TERM/SHORT-TERM ORIENTATION

From an ethical perspective, this dimension could manifest itself in the need to reach short-term earnings. For example, if a multinational accounting firm rewards billable hours in short-term orientated cultures, auditors might have to cut corners to achieve this figure (Marxen 1990; Alderman and Deitrick 1982). This short-run orientation could lead the local office of the firm to cut back on employee training and development, all of which will be detrimental in the long run. This is an ethical concern as well as a behavioral issue because the notion of competence is embedded in all codes of professional conduct. Moreover, the notion of "keeping up with the Joneses" which is evident in short-term cultures could lead auditors to be overly aggressive in soliciting clients in order to support a socially desirable lifestyle. In fact, some accounting firms have become particularly sensitive to protecting the firm from eager auditors' signing on risky clients and require a stringent review process that includes signoffs at increasingly higher authority levels as new accounts are deemed more marginal.

IMPLICATIONS FOR CONTROL SYSTEMS OF MULTINATIONAL PUBLIC ACCOUNTING FIRMS

This paper argues that there is a need to consider cross-cultural issues explicitly when evaluating ethics in a multinational public accounting firm. We contend that an understanding of differences in cultural values can help explain why responses to ethical dilemmas vary between countries. Cultural differences add complexity to organizational control in multinational accounting firms. Firms attempt to standardize auditing practices and client relations around the world by rotating employees to overseas offices, by training programs, and by frequent visits of corporate management to local offices to promote and intensify the tone of consistency and to review the actual status of this effort. Additional efforts to catalogue and respond to cultural differences through both training sessions and the design of control systems are necessary to enhance the effectiveness of organizational control.

This paper provides insight into the reasons why particular actions, seen as unethical from a Judaeo-Christian perspective, might be seen as ethical from say a Confucian culture, and vice versa. We have argued that the first step in building an effective system of multinational organizational control is an understanding of the existence and nature of cultural diversity within the organization across national boundaries. The second step for the audit firm is to develop a control system that reflects this diversity. Hofstede argues that "accounting and management control systems are manifestations of culture and reflect basic cultural assumptions" (1991, 155). Managers of accounting firms could use knowledge of cultural differences to predict where specific parts of a firm-wide code of conduct would conflict with cultural norms in a given country. Table 1 lists the different cultural values and related potential ethical behaviors that would be at variance with the norms within a multinational auditing firm. Note that for three of the cultural values, we are unable to identify unethical behavior for one end of the continuum. Perhaps the characteristics demonstrated at these ends of the three dimensions can even be helpful in designing effective control systems for multinational accounting firms. For example, Hofstede discusses the link between the long-term perspective and an entrepreneurial risk-taking perspective needed in the current competitive global economy. One implication of this for auditing firms is the need to empower workers to take responsibility for quality (including an ethical service, the cornerstone of the audit). Recent interest (e.g., Johnson 1992) in collaborative problem solving as one means of effective organizational control may include characteristics from these ends of the cultural dimensions.

Another control system issue pertains to those countries at the extremes of the cultural value continuums. For example, Hofstede argues that firms from countries where power distance is smaller can manage efficiently in countries where power distance is larger by ensuring that the local manager adopts a more authoritarian style. He notes that firms from large power distance countries have not produced multinational organizations which have had to operate in low power distance countries. Therefore, we have limited data on the implications for North American firms with operations in those northern European countries which demonstrate even less power distance. What issues does this difference raise for organizational control and especially ethical questions? Differences in uncertainty avoidance also create problems for the management of international audits. These problems revolve around the meaning of rules. Individuals from weak uncertainty avoidance countries like Sweden feel uncomfortable with rules, whereas those from Latin American countries basically require a system of specified regulations. In general, local offices in strong uncertainty avoidance countries should institute control systems that are much more detailed and rule-specific than offices located in weak uncertainty avoidance countries. This has implications for the specificity of codes of ethics. Should an accounting firm develop a general code that calls for conduct according to a standard without detailed specifications, or should the firm develop an extensive set of prescriptions in dealing with various constituencies in a multitude of situations to anticipate as many potential ethical conflicts as possible?

Hofstede provides some additional suggestions for implementing an effective international control system. He suggests that two roles are crucial. The *country unit manager* should be a local citizen who is adept at functioning in at least two cultures: the corporate culture as well as that of the business unit. Second, the *corporate diplomat* will be "Home country or other nationals impregnated with the corporate culture, multilingual, from various occupational backgrounds, and experienced in living and functioning in various foreign cultures" (Hofstede 1991, 230). These individuals will act as liaisons, strengthening the corporate-local office linkages in the auditing firm.

TABLE 1
Cultural Values and Potential Negative Ethical Conflicts

Cultural Value	Possible Negative Ethical Behavior
Uncertainty Avoidance	
— Weak	— Failure to accept consistent procedures
— Strong	— Focus on rules to the exclusion of asking whether the procedure leads to an ethical outcome
Individualist/Collectivist	
— Individualist	— Failure to appreciate the existence and the efficacy of the self-correcting mechanism of family face
— Collectivist	— Failure to "blow the whistle" on a member of the group to force a correction of the problem in a timely manner
Masculinity/Femininity	
— Masculinity	— Focus on aggressive client generation and retention that may compromise the firm
— Femininity	— NA
Power Distance	
— Large	— Failure to follow the spirit of the law
— Small	— NA (Note this is somewhat less applicable in accounting firms using a pyramid style of organization which reflects a high power distance decision style.)
Short-/Long-Term Perspective	
— Short	— Short-cuts to achieve performance goals
— Long	— NA

The impact of varying cultures also reinforces the need for extensive use of expatriate manager training by accounting firms. If we expect local economic interests and viewpoints to be subsumed under global corporate objectives, then the organization must build a basis for understanding through interaction and communication. The idea of exchanging managers across country borders is hardly a new one for accounting firms. However, firms need to resolve the negative consequences of international assignments, at least for US professionals. Some accounting firms, no less than other US organizations, have traditionally had difficulty in managing the careers of those returning managers who have taken themselves out of the local US office's career path to work abroad.[6] Often, when these individuals return to the US they experience difficulty in rejoining their local office. Naturally, this can be expected to dampen the willingness of promising individuals to pursue such a career-threatening course of action. The reluctance of some host offices to heavily recruit women accounting managers also needs to be addressed.

CONCLUSION

This paper suggests a need for multinational public accounting firms to specifically consider the impact of international cultural diversity on employee ethical sensitivity and decision-making. Future research should

[6]Based on conversations with a former Big Six partner.

gather empirical data to test specific hypotheses relating to the impact of these cultural factors on auditor ethics. For example, consider a scenario in which a major client of a competitor appears to be unhappy with its auditors. A partner determines that the client's management puts a heavy emphasis on having an upward trend in reported earnings, takes an aggressive approach to recognizing earnings, and top executive compensation is based in large part on the earnings figure. Would audit partners from different cultures differ in their willingness to bid actively for the client? Information like this would allow firms to evaluate (1) whether there is a need to adapt or develop company codes of ethics and/or the ethical dimensions of their audit manuals and training programs, and (2) if change is needed, in what ways. Awareness of cultural differences will help firms to refine their reward/motivation systems to better ensure individual ethical behavior that is in accordance with firm-wide ethical policy. Only by integrating and incorporating cultural issues within the control system will multinational public accounting firms achieve the worldwide ethical standards necessary to ensure the firm's and the profession's credibility.

REFERENCES

Alderman, C. W., and J. W. Deitrick. 1982. Auditors' Perception of Time Budget Pressures and Premature Signoff: A Replication and Extension. *Auditing: A Journal of Practice & Theory* (Winter): 54-68.

Auditing Practices Board. 1992. *The Future Development of Auditing: A Paper to Promote Public Debate.* Consultative Committee of Accountancy Bodies. London, U.K.

Becker, H., and D. Fritsche. 1987. Business Ethics: A Cross-Cultural Comparison of Managers' Attitudes. *Journal of Business Ethics* 6: 289-295.

Betz, M., L. O'Connell, and J. M. Shepard. 1989. Gender Difference in Proclivity for Unethical Behavior. *Journal of Business Ethics* 8: 321-324.

Cohen, J. R., L. W. Pant, and D. J. Sharp. 1992. Cultural and Socioeconomic Constraints on International Codes of Ethics: Lessons From Accounting. *Journal of Business Ethics* 11: 687-700.

Cohn, C. 1991. Chiefs or Indians—Women in Accountancy. *Australian Accountant* (December): 20-30.

Cushing, B. E., and K. J. Loebbecke. 1986. Comparison of Audit Methodologies of Large Accounting Firms. *Studies in Accounting Research #26.* Sarasota, Fl: American Accounting Association.

deTocqueville, A. 1956. *Democracy in America.* New York: Mentor Books.

Dubinsky, A., M. Jolson, M. Kotabe, and C. Lim. 1991. A Cross-National Investigation of Industrial Salespeople's Ethical Perceptions. *Journal of International Business Studies* 22 (4): 651-670.

Frucot, V., and W. T. Shearon. 1991. Budgetary Participation, Locus of Control, and Mexican Managerial Performance and Job Satisfaction. *The Accounting Review* (January): 80-99.

Gilligan, C. 1982. *In a Different Voice.* Cambridge, MA: Harvard University Press.

Harris, J. R. 1990. Ethical Values of Individuals at Different Levels in the Organizational Hierarchy of a Single Firm. *Journal of Business Ethics* 9: 741-750.

Harrison, G. L. 1992. The Cross-Cultural Generalizability of the Relation Between Participation, Budget Emphasis and Job Related Attitudes. *Accounting, Organizations and Society* 17: 1-15.

Hofstede, G. 1980. *Culture's Consequences.* Beverly Hills, CA: Sage Publications.

———. 1991. *Cultures and Organizations: Software of the Mind.* New York: McGraw Hill.

———, and M. Bond. 1988. The Confucian Connection: From Cultural Roots to Economic Growth. *Organizational Dynamics* 4: 5-21.

International Federation of Accountants. 1990. *Guideline on Ethics for Professional Accountants.* New York.

———. 1992. *Professional Ethics for Accountants: The Educational Challenge and Practical Application Exposure Draft.* New York.

Johnson, T. J. 1992. *Relevance Regained.* New York: The Free Press.

Langlois, C., and B. Schlegelmilch. 1990. Do Corporate Codes of Ethics Reflect National Character? Evidence from Europe and the United States. *Journal of International Business Studies* 21 (4): 519-539.

Lee, C., and R. T. Green. 1991. Cross Cultural Examination of the Fishbein Behavioral Intentions Model. *Journal of International Business Studies* (Second Quarter): 289-305.

Marxen, D. E. 1990. A Behavioral Investigation of Time Budget Preparation in a Competitive Audit Environment. *Accounting Horizons* 4 (June): 47-57.

McKinnon, J. 1984. Cultural Constraints on Audit Independence in Japan. *The International Journal of Accounting* (Fall): 17-43.

Ponemon, L. A. 1992. Auditor Underreporting of Time and Moral Reasoning: An Experimental Lab Study. *Contemporary Accounting Research*: 171-189.

Purvis, S. E. C., H. Gernon, and M. A. Diamond. 1991. The IASC and Its Comparability Project: Prerequisites For Success. *Accounting Horizons* 5: 25-44.

Rosner, J. 1990. Ways Women Lead. *Harvard Business Review* (November-December): 119-125.

Soeters, J., and V. Schreuder. 1988. The Interaction Between National and Organizational Cultures in Accounting Firms. *Accounting Organizations and Society* 13: 75-86.

Tsalikis, J., and O. Nwachukwu. 1991. A Comparison of Nigerian to American Views of Bribery and Extortion in International Commerce. *Journal of Business Ethics* 10: 85-98.

Warren, C. S., and J. E. Wilkerson. 1988. Lowballing—An Independence Issue. *The CPA Journal* (January): 13-15.

Whipple, T. W., and D. F. Swords. 1992. Business Ethics Judgments: A Cross-Cultural Comparison. *Journal of Business Ethics* 11: 671-678.

3

Cultural Determinism and Professional Self-Regulation

INTRODUCTION

Regulation is essential to both the accounting discipline and the accounting profession. It allows for an orderly organization as well as the legitimization of the discipline and the profession. However, regulation of both the accounting discipline and profession differ among countries. This chapter examines specifically the differences in the professional self-regulation among countries and uses a cultural thesis to explain these differences.

ACCOUNTING REGULATION IN THE UNITED STATES

Theories of Regulation

Regulation is generally assumed to be acquired by a given industry and is designed and operated primarily for its benefit. There are two major categories of theories of regulation of a given industry: (1) public-interest theories and (2) interest-group or capture theories.

The public-interest theories of regulation maintain that regulation is supplied in response to the demand of the public for the correction of inefficient or inequitable market prices. They are instituted primarily for the protection and benefit of the general public.

The interest-group or capture theories of regulation maintain that regulation is supplied in response to the demands of special-interest groups in order to maximize the income of their members. The main versions of this theory are (1) the political ruling-elite theory of regulation and (2) the economic theory of regulation.

The political ruling-elite theory concerns the use of political power to gain regulatory control; the economic theory concerns economic power.

Which of these theories better describes accounting standard setting? Unfortunately, the theory of what constitutes maximizing behavior in an accounting regulatory agency is in its infancy.

Is There a Need to Regulate Accounting?

A debate exists as to whether accounting should or should not be regulated.

Those arguing for an unregulated market use agency thereby to question why incentives should exist for reliable and voluntary reporting to owners. To solve the conflict between owners and managers, financial reporting is used to monitor employment contracts, to judge and reward managers. In addition, firms have an incentive to report voluntarily to the capital market because they compete for resources with other firms in a competitive capital market, and failure to report might be interpreted as bad news. Even if firms do not report voluntarily, those seeking the information may resort to private contractors for the information.

Those arguing for a regulated market use a public interest argument. Basically, either market failures or the need to achieve social goals dictate a regulation of accounting. Market failures, as suboptimal allocation of issuances, may be the result of:

1. a firm's reluctance to disclose information about itself, as it is a monopoly supplier of information about itself;
2. the occurrence of fraud;
3. the underproduction of accounting information as a public good.

The need to achieve desired social goals also argues for a regulation of accounting. These goals include fairness of reporting, information symmetry, and the protection of investors, to name only a few.

While the debate on the benefits and limitations of regulation continue, standard-setting is a reality of the accounting environment. The advantages and limitations of various forms of standard-setting—regulatory or nonregulatory—may be assessed as a way of improving the process. In the following section, each of the approaches to standard-setting will be examined.

The Free-Market Approach

The free-market approach to the production of accounting standards starts from the basic assumption that accounting information is an economic good, much the same as other goods or services. As such it is subject to the forces of demand by interested users, and supply by interested preparers. What results is an optimal amount of information disclosed at an optimal price. Whenever a given piece of information is needed and the right price is offered for it, the market will generate the information if the price exceeds the cost of the information. The market is thus presented as the ideal mechanism for determining the types of information to be disclosed, the recipients of the information, and the accounting standards to govern the production of such information.

Advocates of a regulatory approach (whether private or public) maintain that there are both explicit and implicit market failures in the private market for the information.

In general, explicit market failure is assumed to happen when either the quantity or the quality of a good produced in an unregulated market differs from the private costs of and benefits derived from that good, and the market solution results in a non-Pareto resource allocation. The same explicit market failure is also applied to the private market for the accounting information, with the assumption that the quantity and the quality of the accounting information differ from the social optimum. More explicitly, accounting information is viewed as a public good, and due to the inability to exclude nonpurchasers (free riders), there is a non-Pareto optimal production of the information of firms.

Implicit market failure theories focus on one or more of the following claimed defects of the private markets for accounting information: monopoly control over information by management; naive investors; functional fixation; misleading numbers; diversity of procedures; and lack of objectivity.

Monopoly Control over Information by Management

The hypothesis claims that accountants possess a monopolistic influence over the data provided and used by the market. As a result, the market cannot really distinguish between real and accounting effects, and may be misled by the accounting changes.

Naive Investor Hypothesis

The hypothesis claims that those investors who are not well versed in some of the complex accounting techniques and transformations may be fooled by the use of different techniques by comparable firms and may not be able to adjust their decision-making process to take the diversity of accounting procedures into account.

Functional Fixation

It is argued that under certain conditions investors may be unable to change their decision-making processes in response to a change in the underlying accounting process that provided them with the data. The failure of these investors to change their decision-making processes to conform to a change in accounting methods is attributed to the phenomenon of functional fixation.

Misleading Numbers

Because accounting relies heavily on various asset-valuation bases and various allocation procedures deemed arbitrary and incorrigible, the accounting output is at best meaningless or misleading for the purpose of decision-making.

Diversity of Procedures

Given the flexibility in the choice of accounting techniques used to report particular events and the inclination of management to present a desired picture, the accounting output from one firm to another is less than comparable and useful.

Lack of Objectivity

No objectivity criteria are available on which management can base its choice of accounting techniques. Incomparable output is the obvious result.

Based on these alleged defects, those who favor some form of regulation of accounting criticize the market approach as ineffective and claim that regulation is superior in improving accounting output.

Private-Sector Regulation of Accounting Standards

The private-sector approach to the regulation of accounting standards rests on the fundamental assumption that the public interest in accounting is best served if standard-setting is left to the private sector. Private standard-setting in the United States has included the Committee on Accounting Procedures (1939–59) and the Financial Accounting Standards Board (FASB) (1973–present). Given the FASB is the ongoing, standard-setting body in the private sector, it will be used to illustrate the advantages and the limitations of private-sector regulation of accounting standards.

Advocates of the private-sector approach cite the following arguments in support of their position:

1. The FASB seems to be responsive to various constituents. First, it is composed of members of various interested groups in addition to the public accounting profession. Second, its financial support is derived from the contributions of a diverse group of individuals, companies, and associations. Third, it has adopted a complex due-process procedure that relies heavily on the responses of all interested constituents. Fourth, the due-process procedure generates an active concern about the consequences of its actions on the constituents.

2. The FASB seems to be able to attract, as members or as staff, people who possess the necessary technical knowledge to develop and implement alternative measurement and disclosure systems. As a unit, the standards are more likely to be acceptable to CPA firms, business firms, and external users.

3. The FASB seems to be successful in generating responses from its constituency base and in responding to such input. The volume of responses to controversial topics shows that the constituents have been expressing interest by participating and voicing their concern through at least three different mediums: written responses to a discussion memorandum, oral responses to an exposure draft, and written responses to an exposure draft. Such participation is deemed essential to the accounting standard-setting process.

Opponents of the private-sector approach cite the following arguments in support of their position:

1. The FASB lacks statutory authority and enforcement power and faces the challenge of an override by either Congress or a governmental agency. This situation is a result of the positions taken by Congress and the SEC on accounting standard-setting. Following the Securities Act of 1933 and the Securities Act of 1934, Congress became the legal authority for standard-setting. It then delegated its authority to the accounting profession. Finally, in Accounting Series Release No. 150, the SEC recognized the authoritative nature of the pronouncements of the FASB and at the same time retained its role as adviser and supervisor as a constant threat of override.

2. The FASB is often accused of lacking independence from its large constituents public accounting firms and corporations. This lack of independence translates into a lack of responsiveness to the public interest. This theme gained popularity as a result of assertions made in the Metcalf Report that the accounting and financial reporting standard-setting process is dominated by the Big Eight accounting firms. One way in which this domination may manifest itself is through pressure in the FASB to avoid standards that would involve subjective estimates, especially standards that would require the use of current-market prices.

3. The FASB is often accused of responding slowly to major issues that are of crucial importance to some of its constituents. This situation is generally attributed to the length of time required for due process and extensive deliberations of the Board. The defenders of the Board maintain, however, that these extensive deliberations may allow the Board to correct the unintended side-effects of some of its pronouncements. This brings to mind the additional problem that the proposed standards have a slim change of being implemented without general support.

Public-Sector Regulation of Accounting Standards

Public-sector regulation of any activity is always the subject of heated debate between advocates and opponents. Without a doubt, public-sector regulation has gained a high degree of legitimacy and become part of American and international traditions and legal frameworks. To be effective, however, regulation must ascribe to certain general principles.

Even if all of these principles were met, regulation is still perceived to be suffering from various failures. The zero-cost phenomenon results from the fact that regulators do not bear the costs of their failures. The regulatory lag or nonfeasance results from delays in regulation. The regulatory trap refers to the difficulties of reversing a given regulation. Finally, the tar-baby effect results from the tendency of regulation to expand continually.

Given these strong arguments about regulation in general, what about public-sector regulation of accounting specifically? As we might expect, arguments for and against public-sector regulation of accounting standards abound in the literature. These arguments center generally around the role of the Securities and Exchange Commission (SEC).

Advocates of public-sector regulation of accounting standards cite the following arguments in favor of their position:

1. It is generally maintained that the process of innovation in accounting rests on the role of a governmental agency such as the SEC as a "creative irritant." The implication here is that the SEC is the most important catalyst for change, and that the private sector and market forces do not provide the leadership necessary to effect such change. The SEC has been instrumental in guiding the field from "safe" or "conservative" methods of accounting toward more innovative and realistic methods of accounting.

2. It is argued that the structure of securities regulation established by the Securities Acts of 1933 and 1934 serves to protect investors against perceived abuses. Thus public-sector regulation of accounting standards is motivated by the need to protect the public interest. It provides mechanisms to offset the preparer bias that institutionally exists in the standard-setting process, as well as to offset the economic limitations of investors seeking adequate information. The mechanisms include suggestions through speeches, the exercise of rule-making powers granted by Congress under the Securities Act of 1933 and 1936, the use of a review and comment process, and the power not to accelerate the effectiveness of a registration statement and to discourage accounting applications in cases judged to be inappropriate, given the circumstances.

3. The SEC is motivated by the desire to create a level of public disclosure deemed necessary and adequate for decision making. To do so the SEC assumes the role of advocate for investors and attempts to determine their needs by continuously surveying analysts and other interested users.

4. Unlike the FASB, the SEC is secured greater legitimacy through its explicit statutory authority. Added to that is a greater enforcement power than a private agency and the absence of an explicit constituency that may "feel their particular ox is about to be gored." In short, the SEC is better able to conduct experiments in disclosure policy when they are enforceable and can go uncontested by all participants in the standard-setting process.

5. Some claim that the private sector has to be watched and controlled, given that its objectives may sometimes contradict the public interest. A minimum of governmental intervention is deemed necessary to avoid the extreme and negative behaviors.

There are, however, strong arguments against public-sector regulation of accounting standards:

1. It is generally maintained that there is a high corporate cost for compliance with government regulation of information. The problem is a matter of concern to opponents of public-sector regulation of accounting standards. The financial reports required by the federal government keep increasing to comply with such legislation as the Sherman Act, the Robinson-Patman Act, DOE pricing rules, OSHA, EPA, EEOC, NHTSA, NRC, NLRB, FDA, FTC, ICC, CPSC, FHLBB, MSHA, and NTSB. All of these reports have an impact on business organization in terms of paper costs and in terms of constant changes in organizational structure that cause the formation of new positions or departments. Added to these complaints are the following as yet unanswered questions:

1. What happens to the reports once they are sent to the federal government?

2. Do they end up in some agency's files never to be looked at again?

3. Or is the information from this one company's reports actually used, along with that from thousands of other corporations, to make important policy decisions?

A study of attempting to follow up on some of this information to see what happens to it would be interesting. Perhaps such a study would also give some indication of the possible benefits to society from such information-gathering.

2. It is argued that bureaucrats have a tendency to maximize the total budget of their bureau. Applied to the SEC, this argument assumes that the SEC is staffed with people who tend to maximize their own welfare with no consideration for the costs and benefits of additional disclosures.

3. There is the danger that standard-setting may become increasingly politicized. Special-interest groups may possess the added initiative to lobby the governmental agency for special treatment. Moreover, political appointees may feel that "witch hunts" are necessary to protect the public interest. Another fear is that "uninformed populists" may want some of the action at the expense of accounting standards and the accounting profession.

4. Some have questioned the need for a governance system backed by a police power. It is claimed that such a situation may hinder the conduct of research and experimentation of accounting policy and is not essential to achieve standardization of measurement.

CULTURE AND PROFESSIONAL SELF-REGULATION

Regulation of accounting standard setting and of the accounting profession is recognized internationally as a way of securing the reliability of accounting statements.[1] The type of regulation differs from one country to another, varying in general in the degree of professional self-regulation.[2,3] The hypothesis of the chapter is that these differences are attributable to culture. This argument reflects a cultural determinism in accounting, in the sense that the culture of a given country determines the type of standard setting and working of accounting institutions. This study uses the latter part of the cultural determinism thesis in accounting to investigate the observed differences in professional self-regulation internationally. More specifically, four cultural dimensions proposed by Hofstede,[4] namely individualism, power distance, uncertainty avoidance, and masculinity are investigated in terms of their impact on the degree of professional self-regulation of the accounting profession internationally.

THEORETICAL JUSTIFICATION AND HYPOTHESES

Culture has been defined as the collective mental programming, a part of the conditioning that people of a nation share among themselves but not with members of other regions, nations or groups. Hofstede identified four dimensions (see Chapter 1) that reflect the cultural orientations of a country and explain 50 percent of the differences in value systems among countries.[5]

Four hypotheses are proposed:

Hypothesis 1: The greater the power distance within a society, the lower is the degree of professional self-regulation in accounting.

In effect, the greater the power distance within a society, the greater is the compliance with legal requirements, statutory control and governmental regulation, and consequently the lower the degree of professional self-regulation in general and in accounting in particular. Gray[6] argued that the degree of professionalism preferred in an accounting context would influence the nature of authority for the accounting system. Professionalism works best when there is a preference for the exercise of individual professional judgment and the maintenance of self-regulation. Accordingly, Gray[7] argued for a negative relationship between professionalism and uncertainty avoidance.

Hypothesis 2: The greater the uncertainty avoidance within a society, the lower the degree of professional self-regulation in accounting.

In effect, the greater the uncertainty avoidance within a society, the greater its intolerance of the ambiguity created by professional autonomy and independence and the greater the need to control through governmental regulation. Professional self-regulation in general and in accounting in particular would thrive best in weak, uncertainty avoidance societies which are flexible enough to accept the ambiguities created by the professional autonomy of the profession and to accept living with them. It is argued that in large power distance countries, the accounting system will be used more frequently to justify the decisions of top power holders, and as a tool to present the desired image and to twist the figures to this end. The described scenario calls for weak professional self-regulation and a loss of independence by the accounting profession.

Hypothesis 3: The greater the individualism within a society, the lower the degree of professional self-regulation in accounting.

Professional membership arises partially from the need of professionals to remain emotionally integrated into cohesive groups, like a profession, which protect them in exchange for unquestioning loyalty. In individualist societies, the need for professionalism and professional self-regulation is less pronounced as the individuals claim to be able to take care of themselves.

Hypothesis 4: The greater the masculinity within a society, the higher the degree of professional self-regulation in accounting.

In a masculine society characterized by competitiveness, achievement motivation, assertiveness and the enjoyment of material success, the professions need to be able to protect their members' trade monopoly, achievement, and the nature and quality of their service, hence a strong need for self-regulation. Only then can the profession create the appropriate institutional arrangement to harness both the egoistic motives for career success and altruistic motives for helping others, and to channel them into professionally competent behavior.[8]

PROCEDURES

Methodology and Sample

The dependent variable in this study is a professional self-regulation score. Independent variables were the four dimensions reflecting the cultural orientations of a country: individualism versus collectivism, large versus small power distance, strong versus weak uncertainty avoidance, and masculinity versus femininity.

To be included in our sample, a country must have available data to measure both the dependent and independent variables. Twenty-eight countries met this test. They are shown in Exhibit 3.1.

Variable Measurement

A recent study presented a survey of international accounting principles and techniques and environmental conditions.[9] The first chapter of the Gray, Campbell, and Shaw (GCS) database included questions on influences on accounting development. The extent of professional self-regulation was determined by the following question: "To what extent can it be said that the government keeps its intervention to a minimum relying instead on self-regulation within the financial community (based in professional standards, training, and a high standard of ethical behavior)?" There were three kinds of professional self-regulation for this study: (1) high, (2) medium, and (3) low. For the purposes of this study these levels were coded as follows:

Classification	Professional Self-Regulation Score
1. High	3
2. Medium	2
3. Low	1

The professional self-regulation scores are shown in Exhibit 3.1. The independent variables are individualism, power distance, uncertainty avoidance, and masculinity.

RESULTS AND DISCUSSION

A multiple regression analysis was used to determine the association between the professional self-regulation score with the cultural dimensions of power distance, uncertainty avoidance, individualism, and masculinity. The use of a discontinuous dependent variable, however, creates three problems: nonnormal error terms, nonconstant error variance, and constraint on the response function. When the error term is not normal, the least squares method still provides unbiased estimates which, under general conditions, are asymptotically normal.[10] The solution adopted for the

Exhibit 3.1
Countries and Professional Self-Regulation Score

Countries	Professional Self-Regulation Score	Countries	Professional Self-Regulation Score
Argentina	2	Malaysia	2
Australia	3	Mexico	3
Belgium	2	New Zealand	3
Brazil	1	Philippines	3
Chile	2	Portugal	1
Colombia	2	South Africa	2
Denmark	2	Spain	1
Finland	1	Switzerland	3
France	1	Thailand	3
Germany	2	United Kingdom	3
Indonesia	2	United States	3
Ireland	3	Uruguay	1
Italy	1	Zambia	3
Japan	2	Zimbabwe	3

other two problems was to use a weighted least squares method. Exhibit 3.2 presents the results of the regression.

The effect of the independent variable of power distance was not significant but had the correct sign. The three independent variables of uncertainty avoidance, individualism, and masculinity were significant and had the correct sign. As hypothesized, uncertainty avoidance and individualism were negatively related to the extent of professional self-regulation while masculinity was positively related. The overall regression was also significant (F significant at $\alpha = 0.01$) and the four independent variables explain 51.06 percent of the variations in the dependent variable of professional self-regulation.

Exhibit 3.2
Regression Results

Independent	Intercept	Power Distance	Uncertainty Avoidance	Individualism	Masculinity
Coefficients	3.3909	-0.0068	-0.0206	-0.0215	0.0188
t statistic	5.10*	-0.99	-3.94*	-2.38**	2.74*
R^2	51.06%				
F	6.26*				
n	28				

*Significant at $\alpha = 0.01$

**Significant at $\alpha = 0.05$

The results of the study suggest that the degree of professional self-regulation in accounting internationally is negatively influenced by the uncertainty avoidance and individualism dimensions, and positively influenced by the masculinity dimension. Basically, societies where people are essentially tolerant of ambiguity are collectivist in their relations with others and show a preference for competitiveness, achievement motivation, assertiveness, and the enjoyment of material success, and have strong conditions for professional self-regulation. This result supports the cultural determinism in accounting, and contributes to an explanation of the difference in the degree of professional self-regulation internationally. Basically, cultural differences in the degree of professional self-regulation from one country to another are significant. A universalistic claim is not warranted on the basis of this evidence and at this stage in the development of professional self-regulation internationally. One consequence of this situation is the difficulty countries may encounter in their efforts to harmonize accounting and auditing principles and facilitate the exchange of accounting services internationally. This cultural determinism is not to be taken, however, as a fixed phenomenon. In the long run, people, irrespective of culture, may be compelled to adopt industrial attitudes and behaviors such as rationalism, secularism, and mechanical time concerns in order to comply with the imperatives of industrialization.[11] This competing hypothesis, known as the convergence hypothesis, maintains that basically managerial beliefs are correlated with stages of industrial development.[12]

As a result of these changes, one may expect in the future a convergence toward a greater degree of professional self-regulation in accounting as countries reach similar stages of industrial development. Further research is needed to test the cultural determinism versus the convergence hypothesis by examining the relationships between the changes in the degree of professional self-regulation in accounting and changes in the stages of industrial development internationally.

NOTES

1. J.W. Buckley and J.F. Weston, *Regulation and the Accounting Profession* (Belmont, Calif.: Lifetime Learning Publications, 1980).

2. Ahia Al-Hashim, "Regulation of Financial Accounting: An International Perspective," *The International Journal of Accounting* (Fall 1980): 47–68.

3. S.J. Gray, L.G. Campbell, and J.C. Shaw, *Information Disclosure and the Multinational Corporation* (Chichester, England: John Wiley, 1984).

4. Geert Hofstede, "Dimensions of National Cultures in Fifty Countries and Three Regions," in *Explications in Cross-Cultural Psychology*, ed. J.B. Deregowski, S. Dziurawiec, and R.C. Annis (Lisse, The Netherlands: Soviets and Zeilinger, 1983), pp. 335–55.

5. Geert Hofstede, *Culture's Consequences: International Differences in Work-Related Values* (Beverly Hills, Calif.: Sage Publications, 1980).

6. S.J. Gray, "Cultural Influences and the International Classification of Accounting Systems" (paper presented at EIASM Workshop, "Accounting and Culture," Amsterdam, June 5–7, 1985).

7. Ibid.

8. R.K. Merton, *Social Research and the Practicing Professions* (Cambridge, Mass.: Abt Books, 1982).

9. Gray, "Cultural Influences and the International Classification of Accounting Systems."

10. John Neter and William Wasserman, *Applied Linear Statistical Models* (Homewood, Ill.: Irwin, 1974), p. 323.

11. L. Kelly, A. Whatley, and R. Worthley, "Assessing the Effects of Culture on Managerial Attitudes: A Three Culture Test," *Journal of International Business Studies* (Summer 1987): 17–31.

12. F. Harbison and C.A. Myers, *Management in the Industrial World* (New York: McGraw Hill, 1959).

REFERENCES

Buckley, J.W., and J.F. Weston. *Regulation and the Accounting Profession.* Belmont, Calif.: Lifetime Learning Publications, 1980.

Gray, S.J. "Cultural Influences and the International Classification of Accounting Systems." Paper presented at EIASM Workshop, "Accounting and Culture," Amsterdam, June 5–7, 1985.

Gray, S.J., L.G. Campbell, and J.C. Shaw. *Information Disclosure and the Multinational Corporation.* Chichester, England: John Wiley, 1984.

Harbison, F., and C.A. Myers. *Management in the Industrial World.* New York: McGraw Hill, 1959.

Hofstede, Geert. "Dimensions of National Cultures in Fifty Countries and Three Regions." In *Explications in Cross-Cultural Psychology*, edited by J.B. Deregowski, S. Dziurawiec, and R.C. Annis. Lisse, The Netherlands: Soviets and Zeilinger, 1983, pp. 335–55.

————. *Culture's Consequences: International Differences in Work-Related Values*. Beverly Hills, Calif.: Sage Publications, 1980.

Kelly, L., A. Whatley, and R. Worthley. "Assessing the Effects of Culture on Managerial Attitudes: A Three Culture Test." *Journal of International Business Studies* (Summer 1987): 17–31.

Merton, R.K. *Social Research and the Practicing Professions*. Cambridge, Mass.: Abt Books, 1982.

Mueller, Gerhard G. *International Accounting*. New York: Macmillan, 1967.

Neter, John, and William Wasserman. *Applied Linear Statistical Models*. Homewood, Ill.: Irwin, 1974.

Nobes, C.W. *International Classification of Financial Reporting*. London: Croom Helm, 1984.

————. "A Judgmental International Classification of Financial Reporting Practices." *Journal of Business Finance and Accounting* (Spring 1983).

APPENDIX 3.1
CULTURE AND ACCOUNTING CHANGE:
A NEW PERSPECTIVE ON
CORPORATE REPORTING REGULATION AND
ACCOUNTING POLICY FORMULATION

Abstract

This paper proposes and illustrates a new methodological framework for studying corporate reporting regulation and accounting policy formulation at the nation specific level. The process of corporate reporting regulation is viewed as a social system, and change analysis is used to determine the essential properties of such a system. The framework allows examination of the system's norms and values; the nature of its interdependencies both internally and with other social systems; the factors to which the system is especially sensitive; and the way in which culture influences the form and functioning of the system's elements.

A great deal of contemporary research in financial accounting has focused on the process of corporate reporting regulation and, in particular, on the process of accounting policy formulation. Since the early 1970s, policy formulation has been viewed as a social process; i.e. as the outcome of complex interactions among parties interested in or affected by accounting standards (Watts & Zimmerman, 1978; Holthausen & Leftwich, 1983; Kelly, 1983).

A typical approach in this research is to examine specific instances of policy formulation, particularly the introduction of new or changed accounting standards. Implicitly, therefore, this research is examining not only the process of policy determination, but also the process of accounting change. Some researchers have viewed the relationship between policy formulation and accounting change more explicitly. Kelly-Newton (1980, pp. 31–2), for example, studied the formulation of accounting policy "in the context of engineering social change and gaining acceptance of innovation".

The study of change in accounting reporting is recognized as important in understanding the rationales for the existence and development of accounting. Hopwood (1983, p. 290) notes that

"attempts to understand the process of accounting change are of significance, not least because of their potential to provide us with a very different perspective . . . for understanding what might be at stake in the accounting endeavour". Burchell *et al.* (1980, p. 12) claim that "the roles which they (financial accounting and reporting) serve are starting to be recognized as being shaped by the pressures which give rise to accounting innovation and change rather than any essence of the accounting mission".

This paper proposes a new framework for studying the process of corporate reporting regulation and accounting change. Corporate reporting regulation is viewed as a social system, and change analysis is used to induce the essential properties of that system. We do not seek to identify the properties of regulation systems generally, as these will differ depending on the nation under study (Zeff, 1972, p. ix). Nor do we seek to propose a theory of accounting change. Our framework uses change analysis to reveal the attributes and essential properties of regulation in a specific nation. In so doing, insights into the process of accounting change will also emerge.

The paper is organised as follows. First, we

From G.L. Harrison and J.L. McKinnon, "Culture and Accounting Change: A New Perspective on Corporate Reporting Regulation and Accounting Policy Formulation," *Accounting, Organizations and Society* 11, no. 3 (1986): 233–52. Reprinted with permission.

review existing research which studies corporate reporting regulation using a change framework. Second, the elements of a social system
which we seek to illuminate through change
analysis are identified. Third, the nature of
change in social systems and the value of studying such systems from a change perspective are
discussed. Fourth, the approaches to social systems change predominant in the literature are
evaluated and a framework based on modified
exogenism described and supported. Finally, the
framework is illustrated through the example of
our Japanese study.

EXISTING APPROACHES TO ACCOUNTING CHANGE

Much of the existing research into accounting
change has drawn on the model developed by
Rogers (1962) and Rogers & Shoemaker (1971).
This research investigates the proposition that
new accounting methods and standards can be
conceived as innovations and that the phenomenon of accounting change is potentially explicable in terms of the theory of "diffusion of innovation" (Rogers, 1962; Rogers & Shoemaker,
1971). In this model, a distinction is drawn between inventors and adopters of new ideas and
the diffusion of innovation is regarded as the
spread of a new idea from its inventor. Accounting research which has drawn on this model has
focused on the characteristics of the innovation
(Comiskey & Groves, 1972; Copeland & Shank,
1971; Hussein, 1981), the channels of communication (Hussein, 1981), the change attitude of
potential adopters (Hicks, 1978; Shank & Copeland, 1973) and the role of change agents and
targets (Hicks, 1978; Kelly-Newton, 1980).

This research has been criticised on a number
of grounds, one of which is its reliance on a
model which fails to consider the sociological
variables underlying the channels of communication, and the anthropological variables of culture and values (Nash, 1971, pp. 228–229). The
importance of culture in influencing the process

of accounting policy formulation in any nation,
and in explaining the diversity of accounting
policy across nations is well documented (Hopwood, 1983, p. 289; Schoenfeld, 1981; Benston,
1976; Zeff, 1972, 1979). Yet, the diffusion of
innovation model does not accommodate
explicitly the influence of culture on the process
of accounting change. In addition, the existing
research which attempts to take explicit
account of culture cannot explain the *way* in
which culture influences the policy determination process. The studies by Frank (1979) and
Nair & Frank (1980), for example, support a
statistical association between culture and corporate reporting requirements, yet acknowledge an inability to explain the nature of that
association (Nair & Frank, 1980; p. 442; Schoenfeld, 1981, pp. 84–85).

The second criticism of accounting change
research based on the diffusion of innovation
model is its failure to examine the social source
(or context) of the innovation entering the system (Smith, 1976, pp. 80–81, p. 93). As its name
implies, this model directs research towards the
process of diffusion of the innovation, but not
towards the stimuli which gave rise to the innovation. Yet, the study of change must examine:
(1) how and why the stimulus for change arose;
(2) the mechanisms by which the stimulus was
accommodated to produce the change; and (3)
the repercussions or consequences of the
change. This requirement is acknowledged by
sociologists concerned with social change generally (Smith, 1976, p. 14; Nash, 1971, pp. 229–
230) and by researchers interested in the
accounting change process (Hopwood, 1983, p.
298; Burchell et al., 1980, p. 2).

This criticism has another dimension in
respect of evaluating existing research. Con-
centration on change as a diffusion process
involving change agents and targets leads to a
view of accounting policy formulation as "planned change". This approach is typified by Kelly-
Newton (1980, p. 4), who regards change as
being "engineered" by policy makers. This represents a restricted view of change because (1)
it focuses analysis on change *within* the system,
and (2) it equates change with the process of

accounting policy formulation. Our framework, by contrast, is premised on a more holistic and natural approach to change. By viewing corporate reporting regulation as a social system, policy makers become seen as a constituent part of that system and themselves subject to change. Attention is directed, therefore, not only to change within the system, but also to change *of* the system. The process of accounting policy formulation becomes an outcome of the system, one aspect of the behaviour exhibited by actors within it. Change, itself, becomes seen as a natural phenomenon of social systems, and not solely as a process whereby policy makers obtain acceptance of a particular accounting change.

A final criticism of existing research is its cross-sectional application of the diffusion of innovation theory to single instances of change (Brummet, 1971, p. 225). Understanding the process of accounting policy formulation in any nation requires the study of more than a single instance of change, and more than just the contemporary state of the system of corporate reporting regulation. The need for an historical perspective has been acknowledged by Hagg & Hedlund (1979), Zeff (1980, 1979) and Burchell *et al.* (1980, p. 23). Hagg & Hedlund (1979, p. 138) claim that "the traces of dynamic processes at given points in time should be interpreted as the result of a complex interplay of historical development". And Zeff (1980, p. 15) noted the importance of historical research in relation to "our understanding of the standard-setting process and of the forces which have shaped current practice".

In sum, current research into accounting policy formulation and change based on the diffusion of innovation model suffers from a lack of explicit attention to culture and history, and is restricted by its focus on the diffusion aspect of change and its relative disregard of the stimuli for change. It is these deficiencies that we seek to overcome by building an alternative methodological framework based on change in social systems. We begin development of this framework with a discussion of social systems and their essential elements.

ELEMENTS OF SOCIAL SYSTEMS

Social systems are frequently described in terms of three main elements; interdependence, norms and values, and cultural determinants of behaviour (Eisenstadt, 1968, pp. xvi–xviii). In understanding a particular social system, such as corporate reporting regulation in a specific nation, the task becomes one of identifying the nature of these elements for that particular system.

Interdependence

In terms of Boulding's (1956, pp. 202–205) General Hierarchy of Systems, social systems are located towards the top and are characterized by high levels of complexity and continuous interdependence. Interdependence relates not only to the interactions among the groups which comprise the system (Parsons, 1951, p. 5), but also to interactions between the system itself and neighbouring social systems (Buckley, 1967, p. 3). The importance of interdependence across system boundaries is heightened in respect of systems at the social level because "the higher the (system) level, the more likely the system is to be influenced and affected by events or phenomena outside the system" (Huse & Bowditch, 1973, p. 28).

Norms and values

An essential property of social systems is that they possess values and norms (Eisenstadt, 1968, pp. xvi–xvii). Values may be defined as "a broad tendency to prefer certain states of affairs over others" (Hofstede, 1984, p. 18), and norms represent the values of collectives within the system. This is not to say that a specific set of values and norms is accepted equally by all elements within the system. Different individuals and groups may have different levels of acceptance of the system's norms and values (Eisenstadt, 1968, p. xvii; Dahrendorf, 1964, p. 103), resulting in the potential for conflict between collectives within the system. Additionally, neighbouring social systems (those with which the subject system interacts) also form their own sets of values and norms. Thus, the potential for conflict arises at two levels; within the subject system, and between the subject and neighbouring systems.

Cultural determinants of behaviour

Culture has been defined as a "collective programming of the mind which distinguishes the members of one human group from another" (Hofstede, 1984, p. 13).[1] Societal or national culture is shared among the groups within a social system *and* across social systems within a given society (Hofstede, 1984, p. 15).

The importance of culture as a determinant of behaviour within and across social systems is argued by both Hofstede (1984) and Parsons (1951). Parsons (1951, p. 5) notes that the values of a social system arise from underlying cultural determinants, and that culture defines and mediates the behaviour of groups interacting within the social system.

Thus, if we seek to understand a nation's corporate reporting regulation from a social systems perspective, we must be able to describe the nature of interdependencies and interactions both within the system and between the system and neighbouring systems within that nation. We must be able to describe the norms and values of the system, and the way in which culture influences those norms and values, and mediates the behaviour of groups within the system. We believe that such descriptions of a specific system are attainable by studying change both *in* and *of* the system over time.

CHANGE IN SOCIAL SYSTEMS

The importance of studying change in a social system derives from its ability to reveal the essential properties which characterize the system itself. The relationship between change analysis and system properties is supported in much of the contemporary research into social systems. Eisenstadt (1968, p. xix), for example, notes that "the direction and scope of change

depend on the nature of the conflict generating the change; on the system's values, norms and organizations; on the various internal forces operating within the system; and on the external forces to which the system is especially sensitive because of its systemic properties". And Smith (1976, p. 5) notes that change is focused upon in social systems research either because the study of change is viewed as co-extensive with the study of dynamic social systems, or because change provides the visible evidence of the interaction of constancy and change elements. In this section we outline the nature of change in social systems.

Smith (1976, p. 13) described change as a succession of events which produce, over time, transformation of the system under study through replacement or modification of pre-existing patterns in that system. Nisbet (1972, p. 1) defined change similarly as "a succession of differences in time in a persisting identity."

These definitions are essentially value-free in respect of the direction of change in a social system; i.e. whether change is "progressive" or may be "regressive". Thus, Swanson (1971, p. 3) is careful to distinguish change from progress, which "denotes that whatever came later was better than whatever went before". Similarly, Eisenstadt (1968, p. xxiii) notes the great variety of forms that the change process may take, including total or partial disintegration of a system, the institutionalization of less differentiated systems, or the development of more complex systems of greater differentiation.

These descriptions of change imply that *events* and the *temporal* and *spatial* dimensions of change are critical elements in identifying and analysing change. Events constitute the concrete and incontrovertible substance of the historical record and provide the data for change analysis (Nisbet, 1969, pp. 26–30; Smith, 1973, 1976). However, while change is described as a succession of events, events in themselves do not constitute change, nor do all events necessarily lead to change. The relevant events are

---

[1] Following Hofstede (1984, p. 21), we use the term "culture" in respect of societies, nations or ethnic groups, rather than in relation to organizations within societies.

those associated with a turning point, or occurrences which mark a transformation from one pattern in the system to a new or modified pattern (Smith, 1976, p. 11).

The notion that change is temporal carries two significant implications for change analysis. The first is the determination of an appropriate time span for analysis. In this respect, Smith (1976, pp. 16–18) distinguished among evential (short-term), processual (medium-term) and trend (long-term) analyses. Evential analysis focuses on the day-to-day or month-to-month relationships among events which form a single change in the system under study. Processual analysis is concerned with examining the clusters or sequences of events relating to a number of individual, successive changes. Here, the analysis typically spans a number of decades. Trend analysis is concerned with a more panoramic analysis of the general direction of change over many hundreds of years.

We contend that processual change analysis is the most appropriate for studying a system of corporate reporting regulation. First, it allows a more detailed analysis of specific changes in the system than is possible under trend analysis. And second, it permits generalizations to be drawn about the essential properties of that system. Sufficient instances of change must be examined to support conclusions about the system's norms and values, interdependencies, and factors to which the system is particularly sensitive.

The second implication of the temporal dimension of change is that the analysis of *each* of the successive pattern transformations within the series must be complete. Change in the system becomes change only when the motion of events has resulted in another pattern or form of that pattern (Smith, 1976, p. 11). The time span of any one change may be decomposed into three phases: a *source* phase, encompassing events which activate the system towards transformation; a *diffusion* phase, encompassing events which accommodate the change activating forces and disperse them within the system; and a *reaction* phase. The reaction phase encompasses events which are generated subsequent to and resulting from diffusion phase events and

which serve to moderate or intensify the change.

The notion that change is spatial, i.e. that change is related to some subject or unit located in social or physical space (Smith, 1976, pp. 8–10) raises two critical issues in respect of change analysis, both of which concern the location of the subject system in relation to other systems or units. The first is the locative source of change; i.e. is change endogenous or exogenous to the subject system. The second concerns the impact of the continuous interactions (interdependencies) among systems on the process of change in the subject system. These issues are addressed in the following section.

FRAMEWORKS OF CHANGE ANALYSIS

Social systems' research provides a variety of frameworks to direct interpretation of the historical record within a change methodology. Most, however, derive from two archetypal images: the *endogenous* framework (dominated by theories and models of evolution, neo-evolution and functionalism) and the *exogenous* framework (dominated by theories and models of diffusion). These frameworks are now contrasted briefly and evaluated for their utility in analysing both the temporal and spatial dimensions of change. That is, they are evaluated in respect of their ability to (1) encapsulate the three phases of change (source, diffusion and reaction); and (2) allow analysis of the complex interactions both within and across systems during each phase of change.

The endogenous framework views change as a continuous process which stems from the inherent growth potential of the system. Social change is likened to the slow and continuous growth that occurs in plants and animals. The explanation of change is seen to lie within the structure and functions of the system itself. Exogenous frameworks, by contrast, are premised on the assumption that the explanation of change must be sought outside the system whose transformation is being analysed (Smith, 1976, p. 70). Exogenism is concerned particularly with the influence exerted by neighbouring systems and units on the system under study. Social change is viewed as being the result of factors inseparable from external events and intrusions (Nisbet, 1969, p. 180).

In pure form, neither the endogenous nor exogenous models are capable of providing total explanation of change in social systems.

Exogenous models direct analysis to the potential of external stimuli to initiate change in a system, but they do not accommodate examination of the system's response to those stimuli. They are not able to explain, for example, why some systems are receptive to new ideas and techniques while others are resistant. Smith (1976, pp. 129–130) noted the differential responses of different nations and systems to similar intrusive events such as both twentieth-century world wars, economic depression, inflation and terrorism. And, in an accounting context, Hopwood et al. (1979, pp. 18–19) noted that inflation, while constituting a stimulus for accounting change, is not sufficient to promote an understanding of or to explain the subsequent processes of accounting debate or response. By concentrating on intrusive events acting as stimuli for change, exogenous frameworks focus on the source phase and de-emphasize analysis of the dispersion of change within the system and the reaction to the change of different elements of the system.

Thus, exogenous models do not permit a complete temporal analysis of change. Nor do they permit analysis of the continuous interactions of groups within the system during the process of change. Because they fail to examine differential systems responses to similar intrusive events, exogenous frameworks fail to reveal the essential properties of systems (specifically the systems norms and values) which direct those responses.

Endogenous models are also partial. By relying on the "growth" metaphor and by seeking the explanation of change in terms of the system's internal structure, functions and roles, these models are also incomplete in both a temporal and spatial sense. In a temporal sense endogenous models focus on the diffusion phase of change and devote little attention to the

source phase. The importance of external events as change stimuli is de-emphasized (Smith, 1973, p. 150). In a spatial sense, the assumption that change is explained by reference to the system's internal elements leads to examination of interdependencies among such elements, but not to interactions and interdependencies between the system and neighbouring systems.

The consequence of this evaluation of the endogenous and exogenous frameworks of change is that neither framework of itself allows a complete temporal and spatial analysis of change. Thus, neither is capable of revealing all the essential properties of a social system that we argued earlier as being necessary in describing and understanding such a system. To overcome these limitations, an approach which recognizes and allows explicit analysis of both endogenous and exogenous elements is required. In the remainder of the paper, we develop and illustrate such an approach, which we term a "modified exogenous" framework of change analysis.

ASPECTS AND PROPOSITIONS OF A MODIFIED EXOGENOUS FRAMEWORK

The modified exogenous framework is based on Smith's (1973, 1976) work on social systems change. Our framework is a development and extension of Smith's work in respect of (1) specific aspects of the framework itself (see, for example, footnote 2) and (2) its application to a social unit as systemic as corporate reporting regulation. The framework is termed "modified exogenous", because, although it includes both exogenous and endogenous elements, the former assume temporal and theoretical precedence. Within this framework, change is analysed in terms of four major aspects; intrusive events, intra-systems activity, trans-systems activity and cultural environment. We describe each of these aspects in turn.

Intrusive events

We noted earlier that change is frequently described as a succession of events which produce transformation of the system under study. In analysing change, however, it is important to distinguish among two different types of events; response events and intrusive events.[2] Response events occur within the system and provide the visible evidence of transformation of the systems pattern. Intrusive events, by contrast, are described as change stimuli; events which typically emanate from without the system and disrupt the system's pre-existing pattern.[3] In respect of social systems generally, intrusive events may comprise war, colonization, missionary activities, economic depression, trade and technological exchange, and the international movement of people and ideas.

Response and intrusive events differ on several attributes which are important in change analysis. First, although any one change in the system may be comprised of several response events, each event is discrete, and the change is evidenced by the "chain" of discrete events. Additionally, the relationship between these events and the transformation of the system is usually both overt and direct.

Intrusive events, by contrast, are typically both non-discrete and non-obvious in relation to the change they occasion in the system under study. Although change in the system may be traced to a stimulus such as economic depression or trade and technological exchange, for example, these events serve more as a set of preconditions leading to the chain of response events, rather than as discrete events in their own right. Additionally, the impact of an intrusive event on the particular system under study is rarely overt and frequently indirect. The impact on the subject system occurs not only through the potential of an intrusive event to disrupt the system itself, but also through disruption to other systems with which the subject system interacts.

Cultural environment

Culture is an essential element in our framework for social systems change because, as we argued earlier, culture influences: (1) the norms and values of such systems; and (2) the behaviour of groups in their interactions within and across systems.

Cultural environment possesses two attributes of importance for the analysis of systems change. First it pervades not only the system under study, but all systems within the nation. And second, the cultural environment does not generate events as data for change analysis. It contrasts, therefore, with the interactivity among the structural elements of the system under study, and between the system and neighbouring systems, which do generate events during the process of change. Instead, the cultural environment serves to constrain or facilitate change through its influence on the nature of this interactivity.

The recognition of only one environment (national culture) in our framework is a critical point of departure from much existing research into the influence of environment on accounting practices in specific nations. The majority of this research regards aspects such as a nation's political, legal and corporate elements as environmental circumstances.[4] By contrast, we recognize such elements as interactive social systems in their own right. Like the system of corporate reporting regulation, political, legal and corporate systems also experience change and are also permeated by the nation's cultural environment.

---

[2] This distinction is not drawn in Smith's (1973, 1976) model of social systems change. However, Smith acknowledged, in correspondence with the authors, the validity of this distinction and its utility in implementing the analysis of social change.

[3] It should be noted that while such events typically originate from without the system, they may have their origins within the system. Thus, the potential of individuals and groups within the system to act in innovative, proactive ways, or to seek to redefine their roles or influence within the system, may be regarded and examined as intrusive events in respect of the system as a whole.

[4] See for example Choi & Mueller (1984, pp. 41—44).

Intra-systems and trans-systems activity

Intra-systems activity is described as the interactions among the structural elements of the system itself. Thus, in respect of a system of corporate reporting regulation, it is the interactions among the specific regulation authorities comprising the system. These may include, for example, governmental, semi-governmental and professional accounting bodies.

Trans-systems activity is described as the interactions across systems boundaries; i.e. among neighbouring systems. Thus, it is the interactivity between the system of corporate reporting regulation and neighbouring systems such as political, legal and corporate. In addition, it refers to the interactions across those latter systems.

The use of the terms, intra-systems and trans-systems activity, is not meant to imply a de-personalization of the process of corporate reporting regulation or the actions and interactions taking place in any social system. Trans-systems activity, for example, is used as a shorthand connotation for the human interaction and negotiation processes which take place between the collectivities, groups and individuals comprising the systems themselves.

The modified exogenous framework of social systems change is built on a series of propositions which link the four aspects discussed above. The first proposition is that trans-systems activity provides the critical, associational link between culture and the system under study. The influence of culture is seen to be: (1) embodied in the behavioural interactions among neighbouring systems located within that culture; and (2) conveyed to the system under study through neighbouring system interactivity with the subject system. Trans-systems activity is viewed, in this framework, as an intervening explanator of the relationship between culture and its impact on the subject system.

The second proposition is that systems change is the product of both the intrusion of events and the continuous interactions among the neighbouring systems and the system under study. Intrusive events provide activating forces

towards systems' change and typically occur within the source phase of change. Trans-systems and intra-systems activity generate the form of change within the diffusion and reaction phases. Both demand analysis. The intrusive event must be analysed for the essential reason why it constitutes an intrusion. It is this reason to which we must look in illuminating those exogenous factors to which the system is sensitive. Trans-systems and intra-systems activity must be analysed to illuminate the norms and values of the subject system and its neighbouring systems, and the underlying cultural determinants of those norms and values.

Thus, the framework is developed on the following relationships. The form of social systems change is visible in the response events occurring within the system. These events are generated through interactivity among the groups and individuals which comprise the structural elements of the system (intra-systems activity). The collective and individual responses of the structural elements of the system to change stimuli are circumscribed by the interactions between the system and its neighbouring systems (trans-systems activity). And, as trans-systems activity embodies the influence of the nation-specific cultural environment, that influence is therefore extended to the response events themselves (i.e. to intra-systems activity).

AN APPLICATION OF THE MODIFIED
EXOGENOUS FRAMEWORK

We used the interpretive framework of modified exogenism in an analysis of change in the Japanese system of corporate reporting regulation. We were concerned with identifying the essential properties of that system and with determining the impact of culture on the process of regulation and accounting principles formulation in Japan.

We examined five changes (pattern transformations) in the Japanese system between the late nineteenth century and 1982. The purpose of the remainder of this paper is not to present the comprehensive results of this study.[5] Rather, it is to illustrate the utility of our framework in gaining insights into the properties and cultural determinants of a nation's system of corporate reporting regulation. Consequently, we summarise aspects of three changes only and omit references to data sources. The changes discussed are:[6]

Pattern Transformation 3: The introduction of three new regulation authorities to the system during the allied occupation of Japan (1946–1953).

Pattern Transformation 4: Modification to the audit function in the regulation system through revision to the audit requirements of the Securities Exchange Law (1965–1982).

Pattern Transformation 5: The introduction of the requirement for consolidated financial statement reporting by corporations subject to the Securities Exchange Law (1965–1982).

PATTERN TRANSFORMATION 3: OCCUPATION CHANGE

Nine discrete events occurring between 1948 and 1953 were identified and ultimately related as comprising the "occupation change".[7] These events are shown in Table 1. As a premise of our framework is that response events occur in the diffusion and reaction phases of change, the stimuli for change must be sought prior to the first response event. There must, by our definition, be a source phase and an intrusive event which will typically originate from outside the system.

TABLE 1. Pattern Transformation 3 — occupation change

Event no.	Date	Event
1	1948	Securities Exchange Law (SE Law) introduced, and Securities Exchange Commission (SEC) established
2	1948	Certified Public Accountants Law issued
3	1949	Japanese Institute of Certified Public Accountants (JICPA) established
4	1949	Investigation Committee on Business Accounting Systems (ICBAS) established
5	1950	ICBAS releases A Statement of Business Accounting Principles, and Auditing Standards and Working Rules. SEC releases Regulations for Preparation of Financial Statements
6	1950	Revision to the Commercial Code
7	1951	Revision to the Commercial Code
8	1953	SEC abolished and administration of SE Law subsumed by Ministry of Finance
9	1953	ICBAS made a deliberative council to the Ministry of Finance

[5] The full study is available in McKinnon (forthcoming).

[6] The other changes studied were:
Pattern Transformation 1. The creation of initial systems pattern through the introduction of the first formal mechanism of regulation in Japan (the Commercial Code) administered by the Ministry of Justice (late nineteenth century to 1920).
Pattern Transformation 2. Pattern replacement through the introduction of two new authorities of regulation (the Temporary Industrial Rationalization Bureau and the Central Planning Board) during the decades of economic depression and war in Japan.

[7] The full change actually spanned the period from 1946 to 1964 with the reaction phase encompassing the period from 1953 to 1964. For illustration purposes we examine just the first year of the reaction phase. A full analysis of this change is available in McKinnon (forthcoming).

Source phase. In this example, the intrusive event was readily identifiable as the "international missionary" activity of the allied (primarily U.S.) forces who occupied Japan from 1946 to 1952. Specifically, the allied forces sought to democratize and decentralize the political, legal and corporate systems in Japan, and to "improve" corporate reporting practices. These practices were seen as having "deplorable shortcomings" when measured against U.S. practices at the time.

Significant structural changes to the political and legal systems were effected under the instructions of the allied forces. Prior to the occupation, the political system was centralized and autocratic, and operationalized through a "rule by law". Formalized in the Meiji Constitution of 1889, "rule by law" was characterized by the subordination of the legal system to bureaucratic control. Legislation was drafted, implemented and administered by the ministries; control of the courts of law rested with the Ministry of Justice; the courts had no power of judicial review over the legislative and administrative acts of *Diet* (Japanese parliament) and bureaucracy; and the rights of the individual in law were very limited.

The allied forces required the preparation of a new Constitution of Japan (1946), under which sovereign power was transferred from the emperor to the people and "rule of law" was established to replace "rule by law". Under a "rule of law", the operation of the law is viewed as the joint task of the government, the judiciary, and the people exercising their rights in law. The new constitution embodied "rule of law" by: (1) establishing the *Diet* as the sole law making body; (2) establishing the Supreme Court and granting it administration over the courts; (3) giving the courts the power of judicial review; and (4) establishing justice as the "right" of the individual in law.

The allies also acted to democratize the corporate system by dissolving the monolithic prewar *zaibatsu* and releasing their shares to the Japanese people. Additionally, they sought to establish a sound and democratic securities market that would provide fair protection for the "new" Japanese investors.

Diffusion phase. The first six response events in Table 1 now take on a specific interpretation in light of the essential nature of the intrusive event. The events may be seen as related through their possession of one common attribute; i.e. the accommodation of the intrusive event of imposed democratization and its diffusion within the system of corporate reporting regulation.

Thus, the Securities Exchange Commission (SEC), the Japanese Institute of Certified Public Accountants (JICPA), and the Investigation Committee on Business Accounting Systems (ICBAS) were established as independent, autonomous regulatory authorities. All were modelled on U.S. exemplars. So too were the Securities Exchange Law (SE Law), the Certified Public Accountants Law and the accounting and auditing principles and standards. The 1950 Revision to the Commercial Code was also designed to promote democracy and the rights of the individual in law by strengthening the status of the shareholder.

These six events are, therefore, determined as constituting the diffusion phase of this instance of change. Our framework asserts, however, that the change is unlikely to be complete at this stage. There must be a reaction phase which, although it may prove to contain no further associated events, is more likely to produce events which serve to moderate or intensify the effect of diffusion phase events.

Reaction phase. Events 7–9 in Table 1 become clearly interpretable as reaction phase events associated with the occupation change, once their import is analysed against the original stimulus for, and diffusion of this change. Specifically, *Diet:* (1) abolished the Japanese SEC and ascribed its functions to the Ministry of Finance; and (2) converted the ICBAS (re-named the Business Accounting Deliberation Council) from an independent advisory body to *Diet* to a deliberative council attached to the Ministry of Finance (events 8 and 9). Additionally, *Diet* acted to restrict the rights of shareholders accorded them under the occupation reforms (events 7).

These events possess two common attributes when interpreted against the original intrusive event and in the holistic context of this change. First, no event served to remove or alter the laws, regulations, accounting principles or audit standards which were put in place by the occupation forces to "improve" corporate reporting in Japan. But second, each event served to diminish substantially the democratization and decentralization of the regulatory authorities.

Just as our framework proposes that the source of change lies in an intrusive event, it also proposes that the form of change is directed by, and therefore reveals, the cultural influences on the norms and values of the system itself. Consequently, we were directed to seek an explanation for the form of change in cultural influences. These influences were suppressed during the diffusion phase, i.e. while the nation was under the direct control of the allied forces, but re-emerged following their departure.

From a complex set of such factors which we needed for a full explanation of the form of change, we select one which yielded high explanatory power. This is the Japanese belief in the moral basis of government, which draws from the Confucianist precept of the natural existence of the "ruler" and the "ruled". This cultural attribute was found to underlie not only the norms and values of the political system, but also the nature of interactivity among the political system and the legal and corporate reporting regulation systems. The perceptions held by the Japanese bureaucracy of their duty and superior ability to formulate and implement the law constitute significant aspects of the norms and values of the political system and flow directly from the cultural attribute of the moral basis of government. These norms and values are realised in: (1) a greater level of active involvement of *Diet* and bureaucracy in all areas of social and economic policy formulation and administration in Japan than in Anglo-American nations; (2) a correspondingly less active involvement of the courts of law and individuals exercising their rights in law; and (3) a lesser reliance on inde-

pendent bodies in policy formulation and administration.

The reaction phase events become explicable, therefore, in terms of the persistence of underlying cultural attributes. Although the political and legal systems retained the structural changes imposed by the allied forces, and gave the appearance of greater democratization, underlying cultural factors dictated the nature of interactivity among the systems. A consequence was the re-emergence of the (pre-occupation) imbalance of power between the political and legal systems. Similarly, the culturally driven norms and values of the political system determined its interactivity with the system of regulation and explained the action of *Diet* in bringing the regulation system back under centralized control.

While it is admitted that the occupation change is somewhat unique in that it provided both an obvious intrusive event, and a sharp distinction among the three phases of change, it supports the propositions of, and the insights to be gained from our framework of change analysis. First, it lends support to the proposition that change is activated by intrusive events and that such events are typically exogenous to the system. Second, it highlights the importance of analysing the essential nature of the intrusive event in respect of its meaning to the system under study.

In this example, we were able to interpret each subsequent response event in both diffusion and reaction phases in terms of its relationship to the import of the intrusive event of imposed democratization on the system of regulation in Japan. Consequently, we gained insight into one essential property of that system; that of bureaucratic dominance. We believe this attribute would have been less visible without the intrusive event interpretation, because bureaucratic dominance is not immediately evident in the comparison of the structural elements of the system prior to and after the occupation change. In fact, the reverse interpretation may have been induced from such a comparison because the system moved, in structural terms, from comprising three governmental authorities prior to the occupation,[8] to comprising two governmental and two non-governmental authorities.[9]

Finally, this example supports the importance of examining not the overt structural elements of the system and its neighbouring systems, but rather the nature of trans-systems activity. The occupation change demonstrates that, although political, legal and corporate systems may undergo overt, discontinuous and perhaps rapid change over a specific time span, the interactivity among those systems (trans-systems activity) is subject to much less rapid and less discontinuous change, because it is constrained by, and embodies persistent cultural environmental influence. Focusing analysis on such activity is critical in making cultural influence visible.

PATTERN TRANSFORMATION 4:
THE AUDIT CHANGE

We used Pattern Transformation 3 to show how events occurring during the process of change may be interpreted through the linkage of source, diffusion and reaction phases. That interpretation allowed us to illuminate an essential property of the Japanese system of regulation, specifically the nature and cultural determinants of interdependence *between* the system and its neighbouring political system. We now use Pattern Transformation 4 to show how change analysis may be used to reveal other properties of the system, notably the external forces to which the system is particularly sensitive, and the cultural determinants of interdependence among elements *within* the system.

The audit change, which took place during the mid-1960s, required the analysis of seven response events. Three major response events are listed in Table 2.

Intrusive event. Identification of the intrusive event activating the audit change was again unproblematic. That event was the investigation of the Sanyo Special Steel Company bankruptcy in 1965. The investigation focused attention on the failure of the audit component of the pre-existing regulation system to prevent or disclose the fraudulent corporate behaviour and financial statement manipulation that had preceded the bankruptcy.

Our framework directs, however, that the intrusive event be examined for the essential reason *why* it acted to disrupt the system. An important insight emerged from this analysis. It was not the discovery of audit failure by the regulation authorities which activated the change. Rather, it was the public revelation of, and reaction to the fraudulent reporting and manipulation. For several years prior to 1965, individuals

TABLE 2. Pattern Transformation 4 — audit change

Event no.	Date	Event
1	1965–66	The Ministry of Finance revises the Ordinance on Audit to strengthen the audit duties of CPAs
2	1966	The CPA Law is revised to re-organize the JICPA and to make membership of JICPA mandatory
3	1966	The Ministry of Finance expands its newly-established Corporation Finance Division. A number of inspectors are transferred to the division from the Tax Department

[8] The Ministry of Justice, The Temporary Industrial Rationalization Bureau of the Ministry of Industry and Commerce and the Central Planning Board.

[9] Governmental: The Ministries of Justice and Finance. Non-governmental: The Business Accounting Deliberation Council and JICPA.

and groups *within* the system had been aware of such behaviour in numerous instances of corporate bankruptcy. By contrast, Sanyo was the first case to receive wide publicity, and was used by the domestic press in a co-ordinated campaign against improper corporate reporting. The essential nature of the intrusive event must be interpreted as the disruption to the system occasioned by adverse public perception of the system's adequacy rather than the failure of the audit component *per se*.

Identification of the exogenous stimuli provides an explanation of why the system underwent change. However, it does not explain the form of change; i.e. the system-specific response to the intrusive event. Once again, we seek this explanation in cultural environmental factors.

System specific response. In Anglo-American societies, we might expect a similar intrusive event to bring a number of responses, including: (1) third party litigation and professional body disciplinary action against negligent auditors; (2) increased standard setting activity by professional bodies in an attempt to avoid the recurrence of such intrusive events; and (3) revisions to commercial laws to clarify and strengthen the duties of auditors. By contrast, the response of the Japanese system was far less diverse. Each of the three response events in Table 2 possesses a common attribute in respect of the form of such response; i.e. each served to increase the level of bureaucratic involvement in the administration of the audit function.

First, through the revisions to the Ordinance on Audit (event 1), the Ministry of Finance increased the duties of CPA auditors and stressed the importance of maintaining independent relations with corporate management. Second, events 2 and 3 provided the Ministry with the means to monitor and ensure compliance with the independent audit provisions.

We were able to explain the system specific response by drawing on the premise of the modified exogenous framework that culture influences the interdependencies within the system (intra-systems activity) through its impact on interdependencies across systems (trans-systems activity). We track this process by considering the influence of culture on aspects of trans-systems activity relevant to the audit change.

First, examination of the interaction between corporations (corporate system) and auditors (regulation system) showed that the concept of independence in audit is not an intrinsic part of that interaction. For the first half of the twentieth century, Japanese corporations had been subject only to audit by a "statutory" auditor, who was typically not a qualified accountant and frequently an employee of the company. In Japan, the relationships between employees and their company are determined by cultural concepts of group consciousness *(dantai ishiki)* and interdependence. Group consciousness refers to the tendency of an individual in Japanese society to perceive him/herself in terms of a group location and, therefore, to accept and emphasize the interdependence among group members. A major focus of group consciousness is the corporation. The acceptance of interdependent relationships precludes, in Japan, the type of "arms-length" relationships which support professional and contractual arrangements among individuals and groups in Anglo-American societies. Instead, it produces social values such as mutual help and the protection of mutual interests *(tasuke-ai)* and the internal and private settlement of disputation *(nai-nai-ni-sumaseru)*.

Despite the introduction of independent professional (CPA) audit in 1947, corporate managers continue to regard the professional auditor as an "employee" of the company, expecting him to protect the interests of management and group affiliates rather than the interests of the investing public. Independent audit is inconsistent with the interdependent relationships on which Japanese society is based, and remains an alien construct embraced intrinsically by neither auditor nor manager.

Second, examination of the interactions between individuals exercising their rights in law (an aspect of the legal system) and auditors (regulation system) showed that third party litigation does not operate to instil or encourage independent audit in Japan. The cultural characteristic of Japanese society, frequently referred to as the "lack of rights consciousness", serves to preclude litigation generally. Thus, despite the existence of liability clauses in the SE Law, no third party suit has been brought against an auditor in Japan.

Finally, the nature of interactivity among the bureaucracy (political system) and the JICPA (regulation system) is governed by the relationships between the bureaucracy and "independent" authorities generally. These relationships were seen in the "occupation change" to produce a lesser reliance on independent, relative to government authorities. The cultural determinants of this relationship were also documented earlier.

These aspects of interdependencies across systems (trans-systems activity) translate directly to interdependencies among elements within the system of regulation itself (intra-systems activity). The relationship between the system's elements of the Ministry of Finance and the JICPA is a strong example. Although the JICPA represents itself publicly as an independent association, and there is no overt or documented association between the Ministry and the Institute which would imply otherwise, the activities of the JICPA in practice prove to be substantially controlled by the Ministry. For example, it is the Ministry, not the JICPA, which sets examinations and determines the number of successful candidates for CPA registration. Additionally, it is the Ministry which takes decisions on the suspension or revocation of CPA licences to practice. This supervision pertains despite the theoretical delegation of such responsibilities to the Institute. Thus, the nature of interactivity we observe across systems boundaries circumscribes the nature of interactivity among elements within the system.

The relationship between culture, trans-systems activity and intra-systems activity in determining the form of systems response becomes visible in this example. The cultural inappropriateness of litigation, coupled with the belief in the moral basis of government, produces a mode of interactivity among the corporate, legal and political systems which emphasizes bureaucra-

tic dominance in the administration of the law. Extended to the system of regulation, itself, these environmental characteristics explain a system response which, correspondingly, emphasizes bureaucratic intervention and dominance. Alternative responses, such as increasing the power and status of the JICPA to administer the audit function, or reliance on third party litigation, become recognised as inappropriate in light of the nature of interactivity across those systems, and the cultural influences on such interactivity.

The dispersion of the intrusive event through increased bureaucratic involvement was, therefore, a response that served to accommodate the cultural inappropriateness of independence and the cultural consistency of bureaucratic dominance. By implication, this supports the explanatory potential of the modified exogenous framework; i.e. that differential systems' response to similar intrusive events are conditioned by environmental influence operationalized through and visible in trans-systems activity.

Analysis of the audit change lends further support to the utility of our framework of change in revealing the essential properties of a system of corporate reporting regulation. First, we were able to draw a tentative conclusion about the sensitivity of the Japanese system to public perceptions of the systems adequacy. This sensitivity was also found in the next instance of change illustrated in this paper, and was made possible by the search for the essential meaning of the intrusive event for the system. Second, the systems attribute of bureaucratic dominance, derived from analysis of the occupation change, was reinforced. Finally, this example highlights the importance of cultural influences on trans-systems activity in determining the form of response to the intrusive event.

PATTERN TRANSFORMATION 5:
THE CONSOLIDATION CHANGE

A series of eleven response events spanning a seventeen year period (1965–1982) were determined as associated with the consolidation change. Nine of these events are shown in Table 3. Event 9, the release of Ordinances Nos 28 and 30 introduced consolidation to Japan by requiring that corporations subject to the SE Law submit to the Ministry of Finance consolidated financial statements in addition to their parent-only statements. We use this final example of change to reinforce the ability of our framework to reveal the influence of culture on a regulation system, through the critical intervening explanator of trans-systems activity. Here we are concerned with the influence of culture on the process of accounting policy formulation within the system. Additionally, the example lends further support to the importance of examining both exogenous and endogenous factors affecting the process of systems change.

Intrusive events. Three events, occurring in the early to mid 1960s were identified as disruptive to the Japanese system and as stimulating the introduction of consolidation. These were: (1) the refusal of the New York Stock Exchange to list Japanese companies in the absence of consolidated statements; (2) pressure exerted on the Tokyo Stock Exchange to accept overseas (mainly U.S.) corporate listings on the basis of those corporations' consolidated statements; and (3) the finding of the Sanyo Special Steel investigation that much of the financial statement manipulation had been achieved by fictitious sales at inflated prices between parent and subsidiary or related companies.

The first two of these events caused the Japanese regulatory authorities to realise that the parent-only statements of Japanese companies carried low international status. The third, as we noted earlier, caused a crisis of domestic confidence in the adequacy of the regulation system. Thus, the common attribute of all three events stimulating change in the system provided further support for our inference from the audit change; i.e. that the Japanese system is especially sensitive to public perceptions of the system's status and adequacy.

Process of formulation of the consolidation ordinances. The response events in Table 3 reveal an eleven years gap between the instiga-

TABLE 3. Pattern Transformation 5 — consolidation change

Event no.	Date	Event
1	1965	*Diet* requests the Ministry of Finance to improve corporate disclosure under the SE Law
2	1965	The Ministry of Finance requests the Business Accounting Deliberation Council (BADC) to prepare an Interim Report on consolidated financial statements
3	1966	The BADC reports to the Ministry of Finance and the Ministry releases an Exposure Draft on Consolidation for public comment
4	1966	*Keidanren* reports that it supports the Exposure Draft in principle, but that it strongly opposes the implementation of consolidation in the near future
5	1967	The Ministry of Finance releases its "Opinion on Consolidated Statements", which supports the introduction of consolidation
6	1971	*Diet* calls on the Ministry of Finance to draft the necessary new provisions and revision clauses for the introduction of consolidation
7	1971	The BADC resumes discussion on consolidation
8	1975	The BADC releases Financial Accounting Standards on Consolidated Financial Statements
9	1976	The Ministry of Finance issues Ordinances Nos. 28 and 30, operational from the fiscal period commencing on or after 1 April 1977

tion of discussion on consolidation by the Business Accounting Deliberation Council (BADC) (event 2) and the release of the Consolidation Ordinances (event 9). During that time, the BADC was involved in some sixty meetings and "seemingly endless discussions" over the formulation of the consolidation requirements, yet those discussions were not directed towards resolving theoretical or technical aspects of consolidation in the Japanese context.[10] Rather, they were directed towards accommodating corporate resistance to consolidation and to resolving the conflict existing between the corporations and the Ministry of Finance over the implementation of consolidation.

Analysis of the relationship between culture, trans-systems and intra-systems activity allowed explanation of the protraction of the policy formulation process, and revealed important insights into the properties of the Japanese system.

Culture. We draw on three aspects of Japanese culture here which relate to the values of the political and corporate systems and to the nature of their interactivity. These aspects are the moral basis of government, group consciousness and the maintenance of harmony. The first of these has been discussed earlier as producing a bureaucratic perception of superiority and involvement in the formulation and administration of the law, and a lesser reliance on independent authorities. The second, group consciousness, was also discussed previously as supporting corporate perceptions of mutual protection and the internal and private settlement of disputation. A product of these values is a strong and persistent attitude of corporate managers in Japan to resist public disclosure of corporate activities.

The third, the maintenance of harmony, stems from the duality of *yang* and *yin*; i.e. from the Confucianist idea of complementary forces (lightness and darkness) which alternate with

and balance each other. Confucianism allows no strict "good–bad" or "right–wrong" dichotomies, but emphasizes instead a "balance of forces". This cultural attribute carries significant implications for the process of conflict resolution among influential, competing interest groups in policy and decision making generally. The preservation of harmony emphasizes: (1) the avoidance of open confrontation between parties; (2) participation, consultation and a readiness to extend the decision making process to incorporate a reconciliation of competing interests; and (3) the preparedness to compromise to attain a consensus decision.

Trans-systems activity — the political and regulation systems. The preference of the Japanese bureaucracy for centralized control becomes visible in the policy formulation process. However, it is visible, not in the overt structure of the standard-setting body (the BADC), but rather in the nature of interactivity between the Ministry of Finance and the BADC.

The BADC maintains the independent and broad representational form envisaged by the allied forces when they supervised its establishment in 1948. Its membership includes, among others, representatives of *Keidanren*,[11] the JICPA, accounting academics and the Japanese Stock Exchanges. The Ministry of Finance is *not* represented on the Council. However, by examining the relationship between the Ministry and the BADC, we were able to establish that the overt impression of independence is not borne out in the way BADC operates. First, the Ministry of Finance was found to maintain an influence over the JICPA and stock exchange representatives on the Council. This influence derives from the Ministry's control over the licensing of CPAs and stock exchange members, and from its close supervision of the JICPA. In effect, the JICPA and stock exchange representatives were found to act as experts for the Ministry in the presentation of the Ministry's policy proposal to the

---

[10] In fact, the final form of the Ordinances drew on established Anglo-American consolidation practices, and have been shown elsewhere to be technically inappropriate for the nature of corporate group associations in Japan (McKinnon, 1984).

[11] *Keidanren* is the representative body for the 839 leading corporations in Japan (Dodwell, 1984).

Council.

Second, BADC meetings are held on the premises of the Ministry of Finance, and Ministry officials fulfil the secretarial function for the BADC. Although this appeared, on the surface, to be of minor import, it proved highly significant when examined as an aspect of the relationship between the Ministry and the Council. Further examination allowed the conclusion that the Ministry uses the secretarial function to keep informed of the progress of council deliberations and to provide feedback on their acceptability to the Ministry. Hence, although the Ministry's involvement in the deliberation council appears to be passive, the use of the secretarial function in this way, and the indirect influence over JICPA and stock exchange representatives allow and result in active Ministry representation in the policy formulation process.

Consequently, neither the BADC, nor as we saw in the audit change, the JICPA, occupy the positions of independent status envisaged by the allied forces despite structural forms that imply such status. Their position of subordination to the Ministry of Finance is entirely consistent with the cultural attribute of the moral basis of government, and supports our proposition that cultural factors determine aspects of the policy formulation process through the interactivity between the political system and the system of corporate reporting regulation.

Trans-systems activity — corporate, political and regulation systems. The protraction of the process of formulating the consolidation ordinances becomes interpretable when evaluated against the cultural determinants of trans-systems activity between the corporate and political systems. We noted earlier that the prolonged discussions in BADC were not directed towards,

nor explained by resolving the technical aspects of consolidation. They are explicable, however, as a process of conflict resolution between the corporations and the Ministry of Finance, and as a process dictated by the culturally appropriate mode of behaviour in conflict resolution in Japan.

The Ministry of Finance has the statutory power to legislate the corporate ,disclosure requirements it wishes regardless of corporate opposition. Yet, a close analysis of the policy formulation process revealed a greater concern with achieving a policy that was acceptable to both the corporations and the Ministry, and relatively less concern with the time required to do so. Additionally, the process revealed more concern and preparedness to compromise on the content of the ordinances to attain consensus and implementation, and less with producing a standard that would improve the inherent usefulness of corporate reports for third party decisions. During the process of ordinance formulation, five major concessions were made in response to corporate representation.[12] These were significant concessions, which allowed the corporations considerable flexibility in their implementation of the consolidation requirements.

Our analysis of the process of formulation of the consolidation ordinances from the perspective of trans-systems activity and its cultural determinants allowed us to gain several important insights into the process of accounting policy formulation in Japan. First, it made visible the motivation for corporate opposition to policy which increases corporate disclosure, and demonstrated the considerable influence exercised by corporate representation in accounting policy determination.[13] Second, it confirmed the involvement of the bureaucracy in the system of

---

[12] These were: (1) the acceptance of consolidated statements prepared in accordance with U.S. listing requirements as meeting the requirements of the consolidation ordinances; (2) a materiality clause allowing the exclusion of subsidiaries from consolidation: (3) the omission of the income-based criterion from the materiality clause; and (4) the postponement of mandatory equity accounting for nine years.

[13] The concessions on the consolidation ordinances were attained by *Keidanren* in the face of Ministry of Finance opposition. and with relatively low numerical representation on BADC compared to that of other parties supportive of the intrinsic merit of consolidation (particularly the JICPA, the accounting professors and stock exchange representatives).

regulation in Japan, and showed how that involvement extends indirectly but actively into the policy formulation process.

Third, it revealed that the process of accounting policy formulation in Japan is essentially one of conflict resolution among the bureaucracy and the corporations, and demonstrated how that process is influenced by cultural factors. Resolution of conflict was not sought through conceptual analysis to achieve the theoretically "best" solution, which may have required a dominance mode of implementation. Rather, resolution was sought through the search for harmonious compromises which would achieve and maintain the "balance of forces" between those parties.

Finally, our analysis yielded insight into the nature of the BADC in the process of accounting policy formulation. The BADC was revealed not as an independent standard-setting authority in Japan, but as; (1) a "pool" of accounting expertise for the Ministry of Finance, and (2) a "forum" for the resolution of conflict between the Ministry and the corporations. The BADC, in effect, serves as a critical element in maintaining a "buffer" between the corporations and the bureaucracy.

CONCLUSIONS

The examples provided in the latter section of the paper are an oversimplification of the Japanese study. However, they serve to illustrate how processual change analysis based on modified exogenism allows insights not only into the process of change itself, but also into the essential properties of a complex social system of corporate reporting regulation.

The framework allowed us to overcome substantially the limitations of existing research which studies corporate reporting regulation using a change methodology. First, by analysing a series of changes in the system (processual change analysis), we were able to draw generalizations about the system's properties. Second, by analysing the source, diffusion and reaction phases of each change, we were able to accommodate the requirement of a complete temporal analysis of the change process. And third, by drawing on the concept of trans-systems activity as the associational link between cultural environment and the system under study, we were able to make visible how culture influences a system of corporate reporting regulation in a specific nation.

We do not contend that our method is the only way of examining systems change or of illuminating the essential properties of systems of corporate reporting regulation. However, we found the method to provide both structure and interpretive utility in our study. Additionally, we believe that it has the potential to enhance research into accounting policy formulation by: (1) locating the policy formulation process within a general perspective of systems change, and thereby allowing interpretation of the events activating the process as well as those generating the form of policy; and (2) incorporating environmental influence on that process through its visibility in trans-systems activity. Consequently, we would encourage further research into both the refinement and development of our framework and its application in the study of accounting policy formulation in other nations.

Application of the method offered in this paper eschews quantitative techniques and relies more on the interpretive and synthetic analytical abilities of the researcher. Additionally, the method necessitates a more disaggregated and sociologically directed conception of cultural environment than is typically encompassed within previous accounting research. We view these requirements as strengths, not weaknesses, of the method, and contend that such depth and complexity of environmental and system analysis is pre-requisite to the effective furtherance of accounting research at the nation-specific level.

BIBLIOGRAPHY

Benston, G. J., *Corporate Financial Disclosure in the U.K. and the U.S.* (Westmead, U.K.: Saxon House D.C. Heath, 1976).

Boulding, K. E., *The Image; Knowledge in Life and Society* (Ann Arbor: University of Michigan Press, 1956).

Brummet, L., Discussion of LIFO and the Diffusion of Innovation, *Journal of Accounting Research* (1971) suppl. pp. 225–227.

Buckley, W. F., *Sociology and Modern Systems Theory* (Englewood Cliffs, NJ: Prentice-Hall, 1967).

Burchell, S., Clubb, C., Hopwood, A., Hughes, J. & Nahapiet, J., The Roles of Accounting in Organizations and Society, *Accounting, Organizations and Society* (1980) pp. 5–27.

Choi, F. D. S. & Mueller, G. G., *International Accounting* (Englewood Cliffs, NJ: Prentice-Hall, 1984).

Comiskey, E. E. & Groves, R. E., The Adoption and Diffusion of an Accounting Innovation, *Accounting and Business Research* (Winter 1972) pp. 67–77.

Copeland, R. M. & Shank, J. K., LIFO and the Diffusion of Innovation, *Journal of Accounting Research* (1971) suppl. pp. 196–224.

Dahrendorf, R., Towards a Theory of Social Conflict, in Etzioni, A. & Etzioni, E., (eds), *Social Change* (New York: Basic Books, 1964).

Dodwell Marketing Consultants, *Industrial Groupings in Japan*, rev. ed. (Tokyo: Dodwell Marketing Consultants, 1984).

Eisenstadt, S. N. (ed.), *Comparative Perspectives on Social Change* (Boston: Little Brown, 1968).

Frank, W. G., An Empirical Analysis of International Accounting Practices, *Journal of Accounting Research* (Autumn 1979) pp. 593–605.

Hagg, L. & Hedlund, G., "Case Studies" in Accounting Research, *Accounting, Organizations and Society* (1979) pp. 135–143.

Hicks, J. O., An Examination of Accounting Interest Groups' Differential Perceptions of Innovation, *The Accounting Review* (April 1978) pp. 371–388.

Hofstede, G. H., *Culture's Consequences* (London: Sage Publications, 1984).

Holthausen, R. W. & Leftwich, R. W., The Economic Consequences of Accounting Choice, *Journal of Accounting and Economics* (1983) pp. 77–117.

Hopwood, A. G., On Trying to Study Accounting in the Contexts in Which it Operates, *Accounting, Organizations and Society* (1983) pp. 287–305.

Hopwood, A. G., Burchell, S. and Clubb, C. D. B., The Development of Accounting in its International Context: Past Concerns and Emergent Issues, paper presented at the Seminar on A Historical and Contemporary Review of the Development of International Accounting, Atlanta, 20 April, 1979.

Huse, E. F. & Bowditch, J. L., *Behavior in Organizations: A Systems Approach to Managing* (Reading, MA: Addison-Wesley, 1973).

Hussein, M. E., The Innovative Process in Financial Accounting Standards Setting, *Accounting, Organizations and Society* (1981) pp. 27–37.

Kelly, L., The Development of a Positive Theory of Corporate Management's Role in External Financial Reporting, *Journal of Accounting Literature* (1983) pp. 111–150.

Kelly-Newton, L., *Accounting Policy Formulation, The Role of Corporate Management* (Reading, MA: Addison-Wesley, 1980).

McKinnon, J. L., Application of Anglo-American Principles of Consolidation to Corporate Financial Disclosure in Japan, *Abacus* (June 1984) pp. 16–33.

McKinnon, J. L., *The Historical Development and Operational Form of Corporate Reporting Regulation in Japan* (New York: Garland, forthcoming).

Nair, R. D. & Frank, W. G., The Impact of Disclosure and Measurement Practices on International Accounting Classification, *The Accounting Review* (July 1980) pp. 426–450.

Nash, M., Discussion of LIFO and the Diffusion of Innovation, *Journal of Accounting Research* (1971) suppl. pp. 228–230.

Nisbet, R. A., *Social Change and History* (Oxford: Oxford University Press, 1969).

Nisbet, R. A. (ed.), *Social Change* (Oxford: Basil Blackwell, 1972).

Parsons, T., *The Social System* (New York: Free Press of Glencoe, 1951).

Rogers, E. M., *The Diffusion of Innovation* (New York: Free Press, 1962).

Rogers, E. M. & Shoemaker, F. F., *Communication of Innovations* (New York: Free Press, 1971).

Schoenfeld, H.-M. W., International Accounting: Development, Issues and Future Directions, *Journal of International Business Studies* (Fall 1981) pp. 83–100.

Shank, J. K. & Copeland, R. M., Corporate Personality Theory and Changes in Accounting Methods: An Empirical Test, *The Accounting Review* (July 1973) pp. 494–500.

Smith, A. D., *The Concept of Social Change* (London: Routledge & Kegan Paul, 1973).

Smith, A. D., *Social Change* (New York: Longman Group, 1976).

Swanson, G. E., *Social Change* (Glenview, IL: Scott Foresman, 1971).

Watts, R. L., Corporate Financial Statements: A Product of the Market and Political Process, *Australian Journal of Management* (April 1977) pp. 53–75.

Watts, R. L & Zimmerman, J. L., Towards a Positive Theory of the Determination of Accounting Standards. *The Accounting Review* (January 1978) pp. 112–134.

Zeff. S. A., *Forging Accounting Principles in Five Countries: A History and Analysis of Trends* (Champaign. IL: Stipes. 1972).

Zeff. S. A., Chronology — Significant Developments in the Establishment of Accounting Principles in the United States, 1926–1978, Jesse H. Jones Graduate School of Administration. Rice University, Houston. Texas. Reprint No. 79–7: Reprinted from Lee. T. A. & Parker, R. H. (eds), *The Evolution of Corporate Financial Reporting* pp. 208–211 (Middlesex: Thomas Nelson, 1979).

Zeff. S. A., The Promise of Historical Research in Accounting: Some Personal Experiences. Jesse H. Jones Graduate School of Administration. Rice University. Houston, Texas. Reprint No. 81–3; Reprinted from Nair. R. D. & Williams. T. H. (eds). *Perspectives on Research: Proceedings of the 1980 Beyer Consortium,* 28–30 May. 1980 pp. 13–25 (Madison. WI: School of Business. University of Wisconsin-Madison. 1980).

4

Cultural Determinism and Accounting Disclosure Requirements of Global Stock Exchanges

INTRODUCTION

Research examining the relationship between accounting and its environment has generally relied on disclosure indices based on the disclosure practices of large corporations in developed and developing countries.[1,2] One exception is a recent study by Adhikari and Tondkar[3] that relied on an alternative proxy, the operationalization of listing and filing requirements of stock exchanges, for measuring the general level of accounting disclosure in different countries. Their study examined the impact of economic and equity market factors on the level of disclosure requirements of stock exchanges and found only the size of the equity market to be a significant explanatory variable. This study seeks to extend Adhikari and Tondkar's study by examining the relationship beween cultural factors and levels of disclosure requirements of stock exchanges. The hypothesis of this chapter is that the differences in the levels of disclosure requirements of stock exchanges are attributable to cultural influences.

CONTINGENCY THEORY OF INTERNATIONAL ACCOUNTING

That accounting objectives, standards, policies, and techniques differ among various countries is an established fact in international accounting. Major differences appear to resolve around such issues as consolidation and accounting for goodwill, deferred taxes, long-term leases, discretionary reserves, inflation, and foreign exchange gains and losses. Given these differences, the comparative accounting literature included various attempts to classify the accounting patterns in the world of accounting in different historical "zones of accounting influence." A general explanation for the various zones of accounting influence is that the accounting objectives, standards, policies, and techniques result from environmental factors in each country. If these environmental factors differ significantly between countries, it would be expected that the major accounting concepts and practices in use in various countries would also differ. It is generally accepted in international accounting that accounting objectives, standards, policies, and techniques reflect the particular environment of the standard-setting body. Various attempts have been made to identify the environmental conditions likely to affect the determination of national accounting principles. The major comments may be made about these studies. First, it is implicity assumed that cultural, social, and economic factors may explain the difference in accounting principles and techniques among the various countries. Second, various important environmental factors which may affect business behavior in general and accounting development in particular have been included in these studies. Basically, the system of reporting and disclosure of a given country may be represented as being influenced by the cultural, linguistic, political, demographic, tax, and legal characteristics in a given writing. In other words, based on cultural relativism, linguistic relativism, and legal and tax relativism, the accounting concepts and the reporting and disclosure system in any given country rest on the varying aspects of that country. This chapter examines specifically the cultural relativism involved in the level of accounting disclosure requirements of global stock exchanges.

CULTURE AND ACCOUNTING DISCLOSURE

Culture is "the learned, socially acquired traditions and like styles of the members of a society, including their patterned repetitious way of thinking, feeling and acting (i.e., behaving)."[4] It has been considered an important environmental factor impacting the accounting environment of the country.[5-9] It has also been argued that (1) accounting is in fact determined by the culture of the country,[10] and (2) the lack of consensus across different countries on what represents proper accounting methods is because the purpose of accounting is cultural rather than technical.[11] These arguments reflect a cultural determinism in accounting in the sense that the culture of a given country determines the type of standard setting and working of accounting institutions.[12] This study uses the first part of the cultural determinism thesis in accounting to investigate the observed differences, by Adhikari and Tondkar,[13] in the levels of disclosure requirements of stock exchanges. More specifically, the four cultural dimensions proposed by Hofstede,[14] namely power distance, individualism, masculinity, and uncertainty avoidance, are investigated in terms of their impact on the level of disclosure requirements of stock exchanges. Four hypotheses are proposed:

Hypothesis 1: The greater the power distance within a society, the higher the level of disclosure requirements of stock exchanges.

Large versus small power distance is a dimension that represents the extent to which the less powerful members of institutions and organizations within a country expect and accept that power is distributed unequally. In large power distance societies, there is a tendency for people to accept a hierarchical order in which everyone occupies a place that needs no justification, whereas in small power distance, there is a tendency for people to ask for equality and demand justification for any existing power inequalities. Therefore, the greater the power distance within a society, the greater the compliance with legal requirements, statutory control, and government of the stock exchange. In other words, in large power distance societies the focus on might and power calls for more regulation of organizations and a higher demand for information disclosure.

Hypothesis 2: The greater the individualism within a society, the higher the level of disclosure requirements of stock exchanges.

Individualism versus collectivism is a dimension that represents the degree of integration a society maintains among its members. While individualists are expected to take care of themselves and their immediate families only, collectivists are expected to remain emotionally linked in cohesive groups that protect them in exchange for unquestioning loyalty. In individualist societies, individual interests prevail over collective interests, and the economy is based on these individual interests. The result is a higher level of disclosure requirements of the stock exchange because, in individualist societies, the focus on individual interests calls for a higher demand for information disclosure by individuals.

Hypothesis 3: The greater the masculinity within a society, the higher the level of disclosure requirements of stock exchanges.

Masculinity versus feminity is a dimension that represents the nature of social divisions of sex roles. Masculine roles imply a preference for achievement, assertiveness, making money, sympathy for the strong, and so on. Feminine roles imply a preference for warm relationships, modesty, care for the weak, preservation of the environment, quality of life, and so on. In masculine societies the dominant values in society are material success and progress. There is also a stress on equity, competition among colleagues, and performance. The result is a higher level of disclosure requirements of the stock exchange. In other words, in masculine societies, the focus on success, progress, and performance calls for a higher demand for information disclosure that allows evaluation of these areas.

> Hypothesis 4: The greater the uncertainty avoidance within a society, the lower the level of disclosure requirements of stock exchanges.

Strong versus weak uncertainty avoidance is a dimension that represents the degree to which the members of a society feel uncomfortable with uncertain and ambiguous situations. In strong uncertainty avoidance societies people are intolerant of ambiguity and try to control it at cost, whereas in weak uncertainty avoidance societies people are more tolerant of ambiguity and accept living with it. In strong uncertainty avoidance societies there is a focus on many precise laws and rules that cannot be changed. The disclosure requirements of stock exchanges are expected to be governed by strict rules leaving little ground for innovation and experimentation. Therefore we expect weak uncertainty avoidance societies to be more innovative in terms of the information requirements of their stock exchanges.

PROCEDURES

Methodology and Sample

The dependent variable in this study is the level of disclosure requirements of stock exchanges (weighted and unweighted). Independent variables were the four dimensions which reflect the cultural orientation of a country: these are (1) individualism versus collectivism, (2) large versus small power distance, (3) strong versus weak uncertainty avoidance, and (4) masculinity versus feminity.

To be included in our sample, a country must have had available data to measure both the dependent and independent variables. Thirty-three countries met this test. They are shown in Exhibit 4.1.

Adhikari and Tondkar's Disclosure Index

Adhikari and Tondkar's composite disclosure index, intended to measure the quantity and intensity of disclosure required as part of the listing and filing requirements of stock exchanges, include a list of 44 items. An actual score for each stock exchange was obtained by summing all the scores received by the stock exchange for the 44 information items that are required by the stock exchange as part of its listing and filing re-

Exhibit 4.1
Countries and Data

Stock Exchange (Country)	Disclosure Scores		Cultural Scores			
	Weighted	Unweighted	PDI	INV	MAS	UNA
1. Sydney (Australia)	74.60	74.64	36	90	61	51
2. Vienna (Austria)	54.17	53.52	11	55	79	70
3. Rio de Janeiro (Brazil)	67.28	68.75	69	38	49	76
4. Toronto (Canada)	79.00	78.64	39	80	52	48
5. Bogota (Colombia)	54.58	54.48	67	13	64	80
6. Copenhagen (Denmark)	67.20	66.86	18	74	16	23
7. Helsinki (Finland)	70.54	71.05	33	63	26	59
8. Paris (France)	76.20	76.16	68	71	43	86
9. Frankfurt (Germany)	67.20	66.86	35	67	66	65
10. Athens (Greece)	60.00	59.41	60	35	57	112
11. Hong Kong (Hong Kong)	77.04	75.77	68	25	57	29
12. Bombay (India)	58.23	58.84	77	48	56	40
13. Milan (Italy)	68.46	68.39	50	76	70	75
14. Tokyo (Japan)	77.68	77.68	54	46	95	92
15. Seoul (Korea)	71.43	72.00	60	18	39	85
16. Kuala Lumpur (Malaysia)	75.69	75.41	104	26	50	36
17. Mexico (Mexico)	70.55	70.68	81	30	69	82
18. Amsterdam (Netherlands)	73.19	72.84	38	80	14	53
19. Wellington (New Zealand)	67.13	65.91	22	79	8	49
20. Oslo (Norway)	60.63	60.59	31	69	58	50
21. Karachi (Pakistan)	55.71	55.82	55	14	50	70
22. Lisbon (Portugal)	65.68	65.50	63	27	31	104
23. Singapore (Singapore)	80.89	80.32	74	20	48	8
24. Johannesburg (South Africa)	74.50	73.48	49	65	63	49
25. Madrid (Spain)	68.84	68.36	57	51	42	86
26. Stockholm (Sweden)	60.54	60.05	31	71	5	29
27. Zurich (Switzerland)	52.24	52.39	34	68	70	58
28. Taipei (Taiwan)	72.19	71.70	58	17	45	69
29. Bangkok (Thailand)	74.78	75.41	64	20	34	64
30. Istanbul (Turkey)	50.68	50.68	66	37	45	85
31. London (United Kingdom)	86.21	84.86	35	89	66	35
32. New York (United States)	90.31	90.75	40	91	62	46
33. Caracas (Venezuela)	73.67	73.32	81	12	73	76

quirements. The disclosure score was obtained by dividing the actual score attained by a stock exchange by the maximum attainable score. To account for differences among user groups, each disclosure score was weighted by its relevance to a list of experts from each of the countries examined. As a result, for each stock exchange, two disclosure scores, a weighted (WTD-SCORE) and an unweighted (UNWTSCORE) were computed (see Exhibit 4.1).

RESULTS AND DISCUSSION

A multiple regression analysis was used to detemine the association between the level of disclosure requirements of stock exchanges with the cultural dimensions of power distance, uncertainty avoidance, individualism, and masculinity. Both a weighted and an unweighted score for the level of disclosure requirements of stock exchanges were used as a dependent variable. Exhibit 4.2 presents the results of the regression.

The effect of the independent variable of masculinity was not significant but had the correct sign. The three independent variables of power distance, individualism, and uncertainty avoidance were significant and had the correct sign. As hypothesized, power distance, individualism, and uncertainty avoidance were significant and had the correct sign. As hypothesized, power distance and individualism were positively related to the level of disclosure requirements of stock exchanges while uncertainty avoidance was negatively related. The overall regression was also significant (F significant at $\alpha = 0.05$) and the four independent variables of the level of disclosure requirements of stock exchanges.

The results of the study suggest that the level of disclosure requirements of stock exchanges is positively influenced by power distance and individualism dimensions and negatively by the uncertainty avoidance dimension. Basically, societies in which people accept a hierarchical order in which everyone occupies a place that needs no justification are expected to take care of themselves and their immediate families only and are tolerant of ambiguity and have strong conditions for extended disclosure requirements of stock exchanges. This result supports the cultural determinism in accounting and contributes to an explanation of the international differences in the level of disclosure requirements of stock exchanges. Basically, cultural differences in the level of disclosure requirements of stock exchanges from one country to another are significant. A universalistic claim is not warranted on the basis of this evidence and at this stage in the development of disclosure requirements of stock exchanges internationally. This result may act against potential harmonization of these disclosure requirements internationally. The differences in cultures create different demands for mandated information by global stock exchanges. This cultural determinism should not be taken, however, as a fixed phe-

Exhibit 4.2
Results of Cross-Sectional Regressions (n=32)

Dependent Variable	0	1	2	3	4	R^2	F
Predicted sign	+	+	+	+	(-)		
WTDSCORE	51.1321	0.2406	0.1863	0.0643	-0.1193	0.2836	2.771**
	(4.778)*	(2.270)**	(2.145)**	(0.826)	(-1.711)**		
UNWTSCORE	50.2165	0.2491	0.1892	0.0575	-0.1114	0.2809	2.734**
	(4.720)*	(2.365)**	(2.192)**	(0.742)	(-1.603)**		

* Significant at $\alpha = 0.01$

** Significant at $\alpha = 0.05$

*** Significant at $\alpha = 0.10$

nomenon. A competing hypothesis, known as the convergence hypothesis, maintains that managerial beliefs are correlated with stages of industrial development.[15, 16] One would therefore expect that as countries reach similar stages of industrial development, the level of disclosure requirements of stock exchanges among countries would tend to converge. Further research is needed to test the cultural determinism versus the convergence hypothesis by examining the relationship between the changes in the level of disclosure requirements of stock exchanges and changes in the stages of industrial development internationally.

NOTES

1. R.S.O. Wallace and H. Gernon, "Frameworks for International Comparative Financial Accounting," *Journal of Accounting Literature* 19 (1991): 209–64.

2. G.K. Meek and S.M. Saudaragaran, "A Survey of Research on Financial Reporting in a Transnational Context," *Journal of Accounting Literature* 9 (1990): 296–314.

3. Ajay Adhikari and Rasoul H. Tondkar, "Environmental Factors Influencing Accounting Disclosure Requirements of Global Stock Exchanges," *Journal of International Financial Management and Accounting* 4 (1992): 75–105.

4. M. Harris, *Culture, Man and Nature* (New York: Thomas Y. Crowell, 1971), p. 6.

5. Ahmed Riahi-Belkaoui, *International and Multinational Accounting* (London: Academic Press, 1994).

6. Ahmed Riahi-Belkaoui, *Accounting Theory* (London: Academic Press, 1992).

7. Geert Hofstede, "The Cultural Context of Accounting," in Barry E. Cushing, ed., *Accounting and Culture* (Sarasota, Fla.: American Accounting Association, 1987), pp. 1-11.

8. Hein Schreuder, "Accounting Research, Practice and Culture: A European Perspective," in Barry E. Cushing, ed., *Accounting and Culture* (Sarasota, Fla.: American Accounting Association, 1987), pp. 12–22.

9. M.R. Mathews and M.H.B. Perera, *Accounting Theory and Development* (South Melbourne, Australia: Thomas Nelson, 1991).

10. B.L. Jaggi, "Impact of Cultural Environment on Financial Disclosure," *International Journal of Accounting Education and Research* (Spring 1983).

11. Geert Hofstede, "The Ritual Nature of Accounting Systems," (paper presented at EIASM Workshop, "Accounting and Culture," Amsterdam, June 5–7, 1985.

12. Ahmed Belkaoui, "Cultural Determinism and Professional Self-Regulation in Accounting: A Comparative Ranking," *Research in Accounting Regulation* 3 (1989): 93–101.

13. Adhikari and Tondkar, "Environmental Factors Influencing Accounting Disclosure Requirements of Global Stock Exchanges."

14. Geert Hofstede, *Cultures and Organizations: Software of the Mind* (London: McGraw-Hill Book Company, 1991).

15. F. Harbison and C.A. Myers, *Management in the Industrialized World* (New York: McGraw Hill, 1959).

16. L. Kelly, A. Whatley, and R. Worthley, "Assessing the Effects of Culture on Managerial Attitudes: A Three Culture Test," *Journal of International Business Studies* (Summer 1987): 17–31.

REFERENCES

Adhikari, Ajay, and Rasoul H. Tondkar. "Environmental Factors Influencing Accounting Disclosure Requirements of Global Stock Exchanges." *Journal of International Financial Management and Accounting* 4 (1992): 75–105.

Belkaoui, Ahmed. "Cultural Determinism and Professional Self-Regulation in Accounting: A Comparative Ranking." *Research in Accounting Regulation* 3 (1989), 93–101.

Harbison, F., and C.A. Myers. *Management in the Industrialized World.* New York: McGraw Hill, 1959.

Harris, M. *Culture, Man and Nature.* New York: Thomas Y. Crowell, 1971.

Hofstede, Geert. *Cultures and Organizations: Software of the Mind.* London: McGraw-Hill Book Company, 1991.

———. "The Cultural Context of Accounting." In *Accounting and Culture*, edited by Barry E. Cushing. Sarasota, Fla.: American Accounting Association, 1987, pp. 1-11.

———. "The Ritual Nature of Accounting Systems." Paper presented at EIASM Workshop, "Accounting and Culture," Amsterdam, June 5–7, 1985.

Jaggi, B.L. "Impact of Cultural Environment on Financial Disclosure." *International Journal of Accounting Education and Research* (Spring 1983).

Kelly, L., A. Whatley, and R. Worthley. "Assessing the Effects of Culture on Managerial Attitudes: A Three Culture Test," *Journal of International Business Studies* (Summer 1987): 17–31.

Mathews, M.R., and M.H.B. Perera. *Accounting Theory and Development.* South Melbourne, Australia: Thomas Nelson, 1991.

Meek, G.K., and S.M. Saudaragaran. "A Survey of Research on Financial Reporting in a Transnational Context." *Journal of Accounting Literature* 9 (1990): 296–314.

Mueller, Gerhard G. *International Accounting.* New York: Macmillan, 1967.

Nobes, C.W. *International Classification of Financial Reporting.* London: Croom Helm, 1984.

———. "A Judgmental International Classification of Financial Reporting Practices." *Journal of Business Finance and Accounting* (Spring 1983).

Schreuder, Hein. "Accounting Research, Practice and Culture: A European Perspective." In *Accounting and Culture*, edited by Barry E. Cushing. Sarasota, Fla.: American Accounting Association, 1987, p. 12–22.

Wallace, R.S.O., and H. Gernon. "Frameworks for International Comparative Financial Accounting." *Journal of Accounting Literature* 19 (1991): 209–64.

APPENDIX 4.1
DISCLOSURE SCORING SHEET

Name of Stock Exchange:_____

Country:_____

General Information	Required	Actual
1. Brief narrative history of the company	3.13	
	----------	= = = = =
2. Statement of Company objectives and mission	3.62	
	----------	= = = = =
3. Description of major plants and properties, including location, function, and size	3.13	
	----------	= = = = =
4. Description of major products, including an indication of those products that are new	3.58	
	----------	= = = = =
5. Information relating to research and development activities including a narrative description of the progress with new product development, and planned expenditures	3.66	
	----------	= = = = =
6. Information on employees such as number, type, and description of employee benefits	2.73	
	----------	= = = = =
7. Dependence on patents, licenses, contracts, where such factors are of fundamental importance to the company's business		4.00
	----------	= = = = =
8. Capital expenditures - narrative and quantitative data on expenditures in past year and planned expenditures	3.85	
	----------	= = = = =
9. Information on corporate social responsibility such as expenditures on environment and community, etc.	2.75	
	----------	= = = = =
10. Extent of dependence on major customers	3.68	
	----------	= = = = =
11. Information on major industry trends and the relative position of the company in the industry	3.89	
	----------	= = = = =
12. Information on the principal contents of each significant contract (not being a contract entered into in ordinary course of business)	3.28	

From Ajay Adhikari and Rasoul H. Tondkar, "Environmental Factors Influencing Accounting Disclosure Requirements of Global Stock Exchanges," *Journal of International Financial Management and Accounting* 4 (1992): 102–4. Reprinted with permission.

APPENDIX 4.1 (continued)

		Required	Actual
		----------	= = = = =
13.	Information on any recent or planned mergers or acquisitions	4.33	
		----------	= = = = =

		Required	Actual
Information on management			
14.	Information on company directors, such as their names, salaries, and major outside affiliations	3.17	
		----------	= = = = =
15.	Information on management, such as their names, salaries, and functional responsibilities	3.16	
		----------	= = = = =
16.	Information on significant transactions of directors, officers, and principal holders of securities	3.33	
		----------	= = = = =

Information about the company's capital

17.	General information on capitalization - designation of each class of stock, par value, authorized capital, issued, and outstanding stock	3.86	
		----------	= = = = =
18.	Summary statement of changes in share capital in past years and any future planned change	3.72	
		----------	= = = = =
19.	Summary of rights, preferences, privileges, and priorities of different classes of stock	3.79	
		----------	= = = = =
20.	Number and types of stockholders	3.00	
		----------	= = = = =
21.	Names and size of stock holdings of largest stockholders	3.59	
		----------	= = = = =
22.	Names and particullars of parties who are seeking to obtain substantial interest (stock holdings lare enough to materially affect control of the company)	3.98	
		----------	= = = = =
23.	Information on any options, warrants, conversion rights outstanding	3.83	
		----------	= = = = =
24.	Historical summary of price range and trading volume of ordinary (common) shares	3.19	
		----------	= = = = =
25.	Information on the loan capital, other borrowings, and indebtedness of the company and its subsidiaries	4.50	
		----------	= = = = =

APPENDIX 4.1 (continued)

Financial information

26. Historical summary of important operating and financial data

3.53

= = = = =

27. Audited financial statements (income statement and balance
    sheet)

4.56

= = = = =

28. Statement of sources and application of funds (statement of
    changes in financial position or statement of cash flows)

4.03

= = = = =

29. Interim reports (quarterly or semi-annual reports)

3.96

= = = = =

30. Information related to post-balance sheet events

4.13

= = = = =

31. Dividend record, including a statement of future
    dividends/dividend policies

3.97

= = = = =

32. Information, about consolidated and unconsolidated
    subsidiaries, including consolidated statements

4.09

= = = = =

33. Information about investments in firms not qualifying
    as subsidiaries

3.44

= = = = =

34. Breakdown of earnings by major product lines, customer
    classes, and geographical location

3.74

= = = = =

35. Breakdown of sales revenue by major product lines, customer
    classes, and geographical location

3.63

= = = = =

36. Discussion of company's results for the past year

3.83

= = = = =

37. More detailed or supplementary information in cases where
    financial statements do not "fairly" present or do not give a
    "true and fair view" of the company's financial position

4.33

= = = = =

38. Information on all pending and potential litigation which has
    had or may have a significant effect on the financial position

4.13

= = = = =

39. Pro forma or "giving effect" statements in cases where there
    has been or is contemplated any major financing,
    recapitalization, acquisition or reorganization

4.25

= = = = =

40. Discussion of significant accounting policies

3.69

= = = = =

APPENDIX 4.1 (continued)

Recent development and prospects
41. General information on the trend of the business since end of
    the last financial year   4.22
                 ----------   = = = = =

42. Any significant information that may affect the market for a
    company's securities   4.30
                 ----------   = = = = =

43. Discussion of the major factors which will influence next
    year's results with special emphasis on the financial and
    trading prospects of the company   4.20
                 ----------   = = = = =

44. Profit forecast   4.33
                 ----------   = = = = =

Cultural Determinism and Compensation Practices

INTRODUCTION

The cost of labor is an important component of the price of products. This cost seems to vary from one country to another. While various economic and social factors may be the reason for these differences, this chapter focuses on cultural relativism as the more important determinant of compensation practice internationally.

COMPENSATION RESEARCH IN THE UNITED STATES

Compensation research in accounting focuses mainly on the determinants of executive compensation in the United States. Empirical research on the relationship between executive compensation and firm performance results from the thesis that such relation is expected if executives act in the interests of shareholders. Several empirical studies of executive compensation tested the relative importance of measures of size, profitability, and return as determinants of executive salaries. The results of these studies are shown in Exhibit 5.1. All of the studies pertain to the U.S. environment. An extension of these studies to the international arena would enable testing the potential cultural relativism in executive compensation. Such researching is important and needs to be encouraged.

Portions of this chapter have been adapted with permission from Ahmed Riahi-Belkaoui, "Cultural Determinism and Compensation Practices," *International Journal of Commerce and Management* 4, no. 3 (1994): 76–83.

Exhibit 5.1
Compensation and Performance

STUDY	COMPENSATION MEASURE	PERFORMANCE MEASURE	SAMPLE	RESULTS
McGuire, Chiu, and Elbing (1962)	Cash salary plus bonus	Sales, profits	45 Large companies 1953–1959	Strong correlation between sales and compensation.
Lewellen and Huntsman (1970)	Cash salary plus bonus plus the sum of all current income equivalents	Sales, profits, and market value of stock	50 Large manufacturers (1942–1963)	Profits and equity market values are more important than sales. The measure of compensation did not matter.
Masson (1971)	After-tax present value of current and promised future returns	Sales, earnings per share, net worth	3 industries, 3-5 top executives for 39 companies (1947–1966)	Firms do have stock market return as a determinant of compensation. Firms do not pay for sales maximization.
Cosh (1975)	After-tax salary, bonus, and estimated money value of benefits in kind	Rate of return on assets, net assets	1600 U.K. companies (1969–1971)	Company size is major determinant. Differences found in quoted v. non-quoted companies as well as interindustry differences.
Ciscel and Carroll (1980)	Cash salary plus bonus	Residual profit, sales	230 large industrials (1970–71) and (1973–1976)	Mixed determinants including sales growth, cost control, and profits.

134

STUDY	COMPENSATION MEASURE	PERFORMANCE MEASURE	SAMPLE	RESULTS
Janakiraman, Lambert, and Larcker (1992)	Cash compensation adjusted for inflation for CEOs	Earnings before extraordinary items divided by average common equity, stock return	609 firms from Forbes Compensation surveys (1970–1988)	Using individual regressions for each firm, they find accounting return has more explanatory power than stock return; including relative performance measures of each of accounting and stock return suggests that relative performance is a negligible factor in compensation.
Clinch and Magliolo (1993)	Cash salary and bonus	Change in shareholder wealth, bank operating income, discretionary income with and without cash flow implications	CEOs from 63 banks (1970–1989)	Compensation is associated with operating income and discretionary income with cash flow implications: also operating income is negatively associated with discretionary income.
Gaver and Gaver (1993)	Cash salary and bonus	Operating income divided by market value of firm	474 profitable firms. 237/237 growth/low - growth firms	Growth firms pay higher compensation and are more likely to have option plans.

Exhibit 5.1 (continued)

STUDY	COMPENSATION MEASURE	PERFORMANCE MEASURE	SAMPLE	RESULTS
Ely (1991)	Change in salary and bonus	Stock return, ROA. net interest income/average earning assets, revenues/average total assets	CEOs from 173 firms (1978–1982)	Accounting and stock return are associated with cash compensation; including industry-specific accounting measures of performance increases explanatory power; accounting variables explain more than stock return.
Belkaoui (1992)	Salary plus bonus and salary, bonus and long-term compensation	Net income, organizational effectiveness, social performance and sales	155 firms from 28 industries (1986)	Compensation positively related to profit, organizational effective-ness and sales. Negatively related to social performance.

STUDY	COMPENSATION MEASURE	PERFORMANCE MEASURE	SAMPLE	RESULTS
Leonard (1990)	Log of salary and bonus	Change in unit sales, change in firm sales, change in profits	Private survey of 20,000 executives from 439 firms (1981–1985)	Finds that hierarchy and other specific firm effects and human capital explain 87% of the variance in compensation, leaving only 13% for performance.
Clinch (1991)	Change in salary and bonus, change in salary and bonus plus change in value of options measured as end-of-year price less exercise price plus the change in long-term compensation including the change in value of restricted stock	Accounting and stock return similar to Lambert and Larcker (1987)	Firms selected to provide cross-section of R & D activity. 303 officers from 116 firms (1970–1985)	After incorporating a separate intercept for each manager, they find that stock return better explains total compensation while accounting return better explains salary and bonus. Further, performance and compensation are more strongly associated for higher R & D firms and accounting return is relatively more important than stock return in explaining compensation for smaller firms.

137

Exhibit 5.1 (continued)

STUDY	COMPENSATION MEASURE	PERFORMANCE MEASURE	SAMPLE	RESULTS
Jensen and Murphy (1990a)	Several. change in salary and bonus; change in total pay from Forbes; total pay plus present value of the change in salary and bonus; the third plus change in value of stock held plus gain on value of options exercised plus change in wealth due to probability of dismissal	Change in inflation-adjusted shareholder wealth, change in accounting profits, change in sales - the latter two apply to only salary and bonus	2,213 CEOs from 1,295 firms (totalling 7,750 CEO-years, also 73 firm subset using Black-Scholes to value options (1974–1986)	A significant but small correlation between the change in shareholder wealth and CEO compensation: the change in accounting profits explains more of the change in salary and bonus. Relative measures of performance explain little.
Kahr. and Scherer (1990)	Bonus, merit increment	"Management by objectives", subjective numerical rating	92 middle to upper managers from a moderate-size production firm (1984–1985)	Managers whose bonus in 1984 was significantly more sensitive to performance performed significantly better in 1985.

138

STUDY	COMPENSATION MEASURE	PERFORMANCE MEASURE	SAMPLE	RESULTS
Barro and Barro (1990)	Change in log of salary and bonus, log of ratio of salary and bonus for current year over prior year	EPS/Price, stock return, each of above relative to a regional industry index	CEOs from 83 banks (1974–1986)	Accounting returns and stock returns contribute equally to explaining cash compensation. Incorporating relative performance does not improve model.
Gibbons and Murphy (1990)	Change in log of salary and bonus, change in log of Forbes total pay, change in log of total pay as determined in Murphy (1985)	Change in shareholder returns, change in ROA	1,668 CEOs from 1,049 firms from Forbes survey comprising 9,245 CEO-years (1974–1986)	Find that compensation is associated with shareholder returns, that compensation is adjusted downward relative to the market return and a one-digit industry return.

Exhibit 5.1 (continued)

STUDY	COMPENSATION MEASURE	PERFORMANCE MEASURE	SAMPLE	RESULTS
Lewellen, Loderer, and Martin (1987)	Salary plus bonus and after-tax related compensation	Proportion of firm's investment opportunities that are long-term, age, stock ownership, dividend payout, debt/equity ratio	5 highest-paid executives in 49 large manufacturing firms (1964–1973)	Found support for mix of compensation components and attributes of firms.
Deckop (1988)	Salary plus bonus	Profit as a % of sales, sales, how CEO obtained position, and human capital	CEOs of 120 firms in 12 industries	Compensation positively related to profit as a % of sales. No incentive to increase firm size. Compensation differed depending on how CEO obtained job.
Abowd (1990)	Log of total salary and bonus, percentage increase in total salary and bonus, log of base salary, bonus as a percentage of salary	ROA, ROE, after-tax operating income divided by total assets valued at replacement cost, annual stock return	99,200 executive years from 225 corporations from private surveys (1981–1986)	Provides weak evidence that increasing sensitivity to performance improves future performance.

140

STUDY	COMPENSATION MEASURE	PERFORMANCE MEASURE	SAMPLE	RESULTS
Gomez-Mejia, Tosi, and Hinkin (1987)	Salary plus current bonus and long-term income	Scale (multiple indices), performance (multiple indices), dummy variable for owner vs. manager control	71 large manufacturing companies (1979–1982)	Performance is significant for owner-controlled firms, while scale is more significant for manager-controlled firms.
Kerr and Bettis (1987)	Cash compensation	Stock returns	129 cases (1977, 1980)	Suggest that neither variation in abnormal returns nor overall market movements influences compensation to top executives
Lambert and Larcker (1987)	Salary and bonus	Change in ROE, measured as earnings before extraordinary items divided by average common equity, stock return	CEOs from 370 firms from Forbes Compensation survey (1970–1984)	Both accounting return and stock return help explain compensation; the relative importance of each is contingent on the noise in each measure, the firm's growth rate, the correlation between the measures, and the CEO's equity holdings.

Exhibit 5.1 (continued)

STUDY	COMPENSATION MEASURE	PERFORMANCE MEASURE	SAMPLE	RESULTS
Murphy (1985)	Several-all measured as natural logs, salary, bonus, deferred compensation, options valued at grant using Black-Scholes model, and the sum of the above	Stock return	461 senior executive from 72 Fortune 500 firms, yielding 4,500 executive-years (1964–1968)	After providing a separate intercept for each executive, finds a positive association between compensation and stock return except for options granted; sales growth is also found to be associated with compensation.
Antle and Smith (1986)	Three after-tax measures: salary and bonus; a comprehensive measure including options valued using a modified Black-Scholes model but excluding the value of shares owned; the second measure including the return on shares owned, less an opportunity cost	Return on assets and stock return, each divided into systematic and unsystematic components using a 2-digit industry return	Top three executives from 39 firms (1947–1987)	Compensation is more strongly associated with relative performance for ROA and is partially associated with relative performance for stock return.

STUDY	COMPENSATION MEASURE	PERFORMANCE MEASURE	SAMPLE	RESULTS
Hogan and McPheters (1980)	Salary, bonus, and contractually obligated deferred compensation.	Sales, profits, vector of personal and human capital characteristics	45 executives (1975)	Sales positively related, profits negatively related. Age variable is significant. Negative for years of service, positive for years as CEO.
Hirschy and Pappas (1981)	Total remuneration, salary plus bonus plus deferred amounts	Net income after tax, total revenues	680 large firms industrials, banks and utilities (1977)	Dual profit and sales incentives exist in industrials. In utility sector, there exist disincentives toward profit maximization.
Agrawal (1981)	Salary plus bonus	Job complexity, employer's ability to pay, human capital	168 life insurance company executives	Job complexity and employer's ability to pay more significant than human capital.
Benston (1985)	Executive turnover	Stock return	Senior manager-directors from 29 conglomerates (1970–1975)	Turnover is associated with poor stock returns.
Coughlin and Schmidt (1985)	Log of deflated salary and bonus divided by prior year's salary and bonus	Stock return measured as annual cumulative returns, sales growth	CEOs from 249 firms comprising 597 CEO-years (1978–1980)	Stock return is positively associated with compensation.

Source: Ellen L. Pavlik, Thomas W. Scott, and Peter Tiessen, "Executive Compensation: Issues and Research," *Journal of Accounting Literature* 12 (1993): 143–53. Reprinted with permission.

COMPENSATION PRACTICES INTERNATIONALLY

Labor cost is a major determinant of the competitiveness of firms in the global economy. Research to date reveals a wide range of compensation practices in different countries within the same industries.[1-5] These variations in compensation practices can be an important factor in firms' decisions regarding new investments on their production and/or distribution facilities, favoring countries with lower compensation practices. An understanding of the international differences in compensation practices can be useful for multinational corporations in meeting employees' expectations about pay equity. Townsend et al.[6] show the differences in pay policies to be dependent on culture, based on the cultural cluster model described by Ronen and Shenkar.[7] While the cultural cluster model has some merits in segmenting countries into culturally related groups for purposes of understanding work values and the relationship of culture to those values, it fails to account for the intracultural differences that make every nation a specific subcultural entity. Following this concern with the level of "national culture," Hofstede empirically identified four dimensions of national value patterns. Accordingly, these four cultural dimensions proposed by Hofstede [8-10] are investigated in terms of their impact on the compensation practices internationally. Four hypotheses are proposed:

Hypothesis 1: The greater the power distance within a society, the lower the level of compensation.

Large versus small power distance centers on the issue of inequality within a society. It is a dimension that represents the extent to which members of a society accept the fact that power in institutions and organizations is distributed unequally. Large power distance societies freely accept a hierarchical order in which everyone has a place that needs no justification, whereas small power distance societies demand equality and justification for any existing power inequalities. Therefore, the greater the power distance within a society, the greater is the compliance with the hierarchical order and the acceptance of the unequal distribution of power, and consequently the lower is the level of compensation. Individuals in large power distance societies will refrain from asking for equality and from demanding justification for any existing power inequalities, which make them more amenable to accept lower levels of compensation than individuals in small power distance societies.

Hypothesis 2: The greater the uncertainty avoidance within a society, the higher the level of compensation.

Strong versus weak uncertainty avoidance centers on the issue of anxiety within a society due to uncertainty about the future. It is a dimension that represents the degree to which members of a society feel uncomfortable with uncertain and ambiguous situations. In strong uncertainty avoidance societies, people are intolerant of ambiguity and try to control it at all cost, whereas in weak uncertainty avoidance societies, people are more tolerant of ambiguity and accept living with it. Therefore, the greater the uncertainty avoidance within a society, the greater its intolerance of ambiguity created by lower levels of compensation and the greater the need to control it. Lower levels of compensation would thrive best in weak uncertainty avoidance societies which are flexible enough to accept the ambiguities created by the low compensation practices and to accept living with them.

Hypothesis 3: The greater the individualism within a society, the lower the level of compensation.

Individualism versus collectivism centers on the relationships between the individual and the collectivity prevailing in a given society. It is a dimension that represents the degree of integration a society maintains among its members. In collectivist societies, individuals remain emotionally integrated in cohesive groups, like union or professions, which protect them in exchange for unquestioning loyalty. In individualist societies, people are more concerned with themselves and their families and claim to be able to take care of themselves. The reality is that the concessions on compensation are best obtained when groups, rather than separate individuals, bargain for a level of compensation. One would expect a higher level of compensation in collectivist societies.

Hypothesis 4: The greater the masculinity within a society, the higher the level of compensation.

Masculinity versus femininity is a dimension that represents the nature of social divisions of sex roles. Masculine roles imply a preference for achievement, assertiveness, making money, sympathy for the strong, etc. Feminine roles imply a preference for warm relationships, modesty, care for the weak, preservation of the environment, quality of life, and so on. Masculine societies are tough competitive societies where individuals place a high value on achievement and the acquisition of money as a measure of strength. One would expect the masculine societies to value a higher level of compensation than feminine societies.

PROCEDURES

The analyses relied on regressions between measures of compensation on one hand and values for the four cultural dimensions of power distance, individualism, uncertainty avoidance, and masculinity.

The compensation measures were derived from a compensation cost report prepared by the U.S. Department of Labor, Bureau of Labor Statistics, Office of Productivity and Technology (1990). The data included international comparisons of hourly compensation costs, hourly direct pay, and pay for the time worked for production workers in manufacturing in 34 countries or areas. Accordingly, hourly compensation costs, pay for time worked, and hourly direct pay were used as dependent variables. They are defined as follows:

1. *Hourly compensation* is defined as (1) all payments made directly to the worker, before payroll deductions of any kind, and (2) employer social insurance expenditures (i.e., expenditures for legally required insurance programs and contractual and private benefit plans). This variable is measured on an hours-worked basis for every country.

2. *Hourly direct pay* includes pay for time worked (basic time and piece rates plus overtime premiums, shift differentials, other premiums and bonuses paid regularly each pay period, and cost-of-living adjustments) and other direct pay— pay for time not worked (vacations, holidays, and other leave, except sick leave), seasonal or irregular bonuses and other special payments, selected social allowances, and the cost of payments in kind, before deductions of any kind. This variable is also measured on an hours-worked basis for every country.

3. *Pay for time worked* includes only basic time and piece rates, overtime premiums, shift differentials, other premiums and bonuses paid regularly each pay period, and cost-of-living adjustments.

These three measures of compensation are measured on an hours-worked basis for every country.

The independent variables were the four dimensions identified as reflecting the cultural orientations of a country.

To be included in our sample, a country must have available data to measure both the dependent and independent variables used in this study. Thirty-two countries met this test. They are shown in Exhibit 5.2.

RESULTS AND DISCUSSION

Multiple regression analyses were used to determine the association between three measures of compensation and the cultural dimensions of power distance, uncertainty avoidance, individualism, and masculinity. Exhibits 5.3, 5.4, and 5.5 present the results of the regressions. The effects

Exhibit 5.2
List of Countries Used

1. Australia
2. Austria
3. Belgium
4. Brazil
5. Canada
6. Denmark
7. Finland
8. France
9. Germany
10. Great Britain
11. Greece
12. Hong Kong
13. India
14. Ireland
15. Israel
16. Italy
17. Japan
18. Korea
19. Mexico
20. Netherlands
21. Norway
22. New Zealand
23. Pakistan
24. Portugal
25. Singapore
26. Spain
27. Sweden
28. Switzerland
29. Taiwan
30. Turkey
31. United States
32. Venezuela

Exhibit 5.3
Pay for Time Worked in U.S. Dollars

Year	Inter-cept	Power Distance	Uncertainty Avoidance	Indivi-dualism	Mascul-inity	R	F
1985	1.624 (1.129)	−0.013 (−0.994)	0.044 (2.639)*	−0.0111 (−0.786)	0.0001 (2.144)**	61.88%	5.682*
1986	1.705 (1.362)	−0.007 (−0.617)	0.041 (2.840)*	−0.018 (−1.492)	0.0002 (4.041)*	76.80%	11.58*
1987	2.859 (1.747)	−0.0044 (−0.286)	0.0399 (2.092)**	−0.0370 (−2.297)**	0.0002 (3.750)*	73.64%	9.779*
1988	3.0087 (1.817)	−0.0065 (−0.418)	0.0402 (2.085)**	−0.032 (−2.003)	0.00032 (4.259)*	75.83%	10.979*
1989	2.186 (1.452)	−0.0048 (−0.339)	0.059 (3.363)*	−0.037 (−2.532)**	0.0003 (4.394)*	81.79%	15.65*

*   Significant at $\alpha = 0.01$
**   Significant at $\alpha = 0.05$
*** Significant at $\alpha = 0.10$

Exhibit 5.4
Hourly Direct Pay in U.S. Dollars

Year	Inter-cept	Power Distance	Uncertainty Avoidance	Indivi-dualism	Mascul-inity	R	F
1985	0.4581 (0.445)	-0.005 (-0.497)	0.0472 (3.6164)*	-0.009 (0.850)	0.00023 (4.738)*	83.53%	26.62*
1986	-0.142 (-0.133)	0.0051 (0.489)	0.044 (3.134)*	-0.0169 (-1.433)	0.00037 (7.297)*	89.00%	42.48*
1987	0.0046 (0.003)	0.0104 (0.742)	0.045 (2.398)**	-0.030 (-1.913)	0.00048 (7.092)*	87.24%	35.907*
1988	0.397 (0.264)	0.0099 (0.670)	0.0449 (2.258)**	-0.0310 (-1.866)	0.0005 (7.197)*	87.27%	35.92*
1989	9.89 (1.689)	0.168 (2.910)*	0.125 (1.621)	-0.099 (-1.529)	-0.00 (-0.716)	36.80%	3.057**

```
*    Significant at α = 0.01
**   Significant at α = 0.05
***  Significant at α = 0.10
```

of the independent variable of power distance was neither significant nor had the right sign. The three independent variables of uncertainty avoidance, individualism, and masculinity were significant and had the correct sign in the three cases and for the five years examined. As hypothesized, the level of compensation, as measured by hourly compensation, pay for time worked, and hourly direct pay, was negatively related to individualism and positively related to both uncertainty avoidance and masculinity. The overall regression was also highly significant for all cases and for the five years examined (F significant at $\alpha = 0.01$), and the four independent variables explain a significant proportion of the variations in the level of compensation (a minimum R^2 of 36.08% and a maximum R^2 of 89%). The results of the study suggest that the level of compensation internationally is negatively influenced by individualism and positively influenced by both uncertainty avoidance and masculinity. Basically, societies where people are collectivist in their relations with others, intolerant of ambiguity, and show a preference for competitiveness, achievement motivation, assertiveness, and the enjoyment of material success have strong conditions for a high level of compensation.

Exhibit 5.5
Hourly Compensation Costs in U.S. Dollars

Year	Inter-cept	Power Distance	Uncertainty Avoidance	Indivi-dualism	Mascul-inity	R	F
1985	0.249 (0.209)	0.0018 (0.159)	0.0639 (4.056)*	-0.0191 (-8.453)**	0.00028 (4.970)*	85.51%	30.98*
1986	-0.757 (-0.559)	0.0187 (1.407)	0.635 (3.539)*	-0.0304 (-2.035)**	0.00045 (7.025)*	88.86%	41.861*
1987	-0.791 (-0.437)	0.0285 (1.599)	0.0671 (2.799)*	-0.0487 (-2.434)**	0.00059 (6.830)*	87.12%	35.50*
1988	-0.338 (-0.186)	0.0289 (1.616)	0.0688 (2.857)*	-0.0519 (-2.582)*	0.00064 (7.292)*	88.32%	39.71*
1989	0.393 (0.231)	0.0262 (1.566)	0.0747 (3.325)*	0.0551 (-2.935)*	0.00059 (7.224)*	89.08%	42.82*

```
*    Significant at α = 0.01
**   Significant at α = 0.05
***  Significant at α = 0.10
```

These results support the cultural determinism thesis in setting compensation practices, and contribute to an explanation of the differences in international compensation practices. Basically, cultural differences in the level of compensation from one country to another are significant. These results are in support of previous findings centered on the Ronen and Shenkar model.[11,12] The results show, however, that there are differences in the cost of labor between countries within a culture depending on the level of three of the cultural dimensions. Labor costs are not only determined by market forces but also influenced by the cultural dimensions of individualism, uncertainty avoidance, and masculinity. The results refute the assertion that employment practices are only marginally affected by cultural affiliation.[13] This cultural determinism thesis is not to be taken, however, as a fixed phenomenon. In the long run, people, irrespective of their culture, may be compelled to provide similar levels of compensation to comply with similar imperatives of industrialization.[14] This competing hypothesis, generally labeled the convergence hypothesis, argues for convergence between managerial practices and stages of industrial development.[15] It calls for an investigation of the relationships between the changes in the level of compensation and changes in stages of industrial development internationally. Another worthwhile avenue of research is to investigate the combined effect of cultural and economic variables on compensation practices internationally.

NOTES

1. Michael White, *Payment Systems in Britain* (Aldershot, England: Gower, 1981).
2. Angela Bowey and Richard Thorpe, *Payment Systems and Productivity* (New York: St. Martin's, 1986).
3. Masanori Hashimoto and John Raisian, "Employment Tenure and Earnings Profiles in Japan and the United States, "*American Economic Review* (September 1985): 721–35.
4. Rosalie Tung, "Patterns of Motivation in Chinese Industrial Enterprises," *Academy of Management Review* 6, no. 3 (1981).
5. James Nelson and John Reeder, "Labor Relations in China," *California Management Review* 27, no. 4 (1985): 13-32.
6. Anthony M. Townsend, K. Dow Scott, and Stephen E. Marrkham, "An Examination of Country and Culture-Based Differences in Compensation Practices," *Journal of International Business Studies* 21, no. 4 (1990): 667–78.
7. Simcha Ronen and Oded Shenkar, "Clustering Countries on Attitudinal Dimensions: A Review and Synthesis," *Academy of Management Review* 10 (1985): 435–54.
8. Geert Hofstede, *Cultures and Organizations: Software of the Mind* (London: McGraw Hill Book Company, 1991).
9. Geert Hofstede, "Dimensions of National Cultures in Fifty Countries and Three Regions," in J.B. Deregowski, S. Dziurawiee, and R.C. Annis, eds., *Explications in Cross-Cultural Psychology* (Lisse, The Netherlands: Soviets and Zeilinger, 1983), pp. 335–35.
10. Geert Hofstede, *Culture's Consequences: International Differences in Work Related Values* (Beverly Hills, Calif.: Sage Publications, 1980).
11. Ronen, Shenkar, "Clustering Countries on Attitudinal Dimensions: A Review and Synthesis."
12. Townsend et al., "An Examination of Country and Culture-Based Differences in Compensation Practices," pp. 667–78.
13. Anant Neghandi, "Cross Cultural Studies: Too Many Conclusions," in A. Neghandi, ed., *Modern Organizational Theory* (Kent: Ohio, 1975).
14. L. Kelly, A. Whatley, and R. Worthley, "Assessing the Effects of Culture on Managerial Attitudes: A Three Culture Test," *Journal of International Business Studies* (Summer 1987): 17–31.
15. F. Harbison and C.A. Myers, *Management in the Industrial World* (New York: McGraw Hill, 1959).

REFERENCES

Abowd, J.M. "Does Performance-based Managerial Compensation Affect Corporate Performance?" *Industrial and Labor Relations Review* 43, no. 2 (1990): 52S–73S.

Agrawal, N. "Determinants of Executive Compensation." *Industrial Relations* 20 (Winter 1981): 36–46.

Antle, R., and A. Smith. "An Empirical Investigation of the Relative Performance Evaluation of Corporate Executives." *Journal of Accounting Research* 24 (Spring 1986): 1-39.

———. "Measuring Executive Compensation: Methods and an Application." *Journal of Accounting Research* 23 (Spring 1985): 296–325.

Barro, J.R., and R.J. Barro. "Pay, Performance, and Turnover of Bank CEOs." *Journal of Labor Economics* 8, no. 10 (1990): 448–81.

Belkaoui, A. "Executive Compensation, Organizational Effectiveness, Social Performance and Firm Performance: An Empirical Investigation." *Journal of Business Finance and Accounting* 19, no. 1 (1992): 67–84.

Benston, G. "The Self-Serving Hypothesis: Some Evidence." *Journal of Accounting and Economics* 7, no. 4 (1985): pp. 67–84.

Bizjak, J., J. Brickley, and J. Coles. "Stock-Based Incentive Compensation and Investment Behavior." *Journal of Accounting and Economics* 7, no. 4 (1993): 349–72.

Bowey, Angela, and Richard Thorpe. *Payment Systems and Productivity* (New York: St. Martin's, 1986).

Ciscel, D., and T. Carroll. "The Determinants of Executive Salaries: An Econometric Survey." *Review of Economics and Statistics* 62, no. 2 (1980): 7–13.

Clinch, G. "Employee Compensation and Firms' Research and Development Activity." *Journal of Accounting Research* 27 (Spring 1991): 59–78.

Clinch, G., and J. Magliolo. "CEO Compensation and Components of Earnings in Bank Holding Companies." *Journal of Accounting and Economics* 16 (January/April/July 1993): 241–72.

Cosh, A. "The Renumeration of Chief Executives in the United Kingdom." *Economics Journal* 85, no. 3 (1975): 75-94.

Coughlin, A., and R. Schmidt. "Executive Compensation, Management Turnover, and Firm Performance: An Empirical Investigation," *Journal of Accounting and Economics* 7, no. 4 (1985): 43–66.

Deckop, J.R. "Determinants of Chief Executive Officer Compensation." *Industrial and Labor Relations Review* 41, no. 1 (1991): 37–58.

Ely, K. "Interindustry Differences in the Relation Between Compensation and Firm Performance." *Journal of Accounting Research* 29 (Spring 1991): pp. 37–58.

Gaver, J.F., and K.M. Gaver. "Additional Evidence on the Association Between the Investment Opportunity Set and Corporate Financing, Dividend, and Compensation Policies." *Journal of Accounting and Economics* 16 (January/April/July 1993): 125-60.

Gaver, J.F., K.M. Gaver, and J. Austin. "Additional Evidence on the Association Between Income Management and Earnings-based Bonus Plans." Working paper, University of Georgia, 1993.

Gaver, J.F., K.M. Gaver, and G.P. Battistel. "The Stock Market Reaction to Performance Plan Adoptions." *Accounting Review* 67, no. 1 (1992): 172–82.

Gerhart, B., and G.T. Milkovich. "Organizational Differences in Managerial Compensation and Financial Performance." *Academy of Management Journal* 30, no. 12 (1990): 663–91.

Gibbons, R., and K.J. Murphy. "Relative Performance Evaluation for Chief Executive Officers." *Industrial and Labor Relations Review* 43, no. 2 (1990): 30S–51S.

Giddens, A. *The Constitution of Society: Outline of the Theory of Structuration.* Cambridge, England: Polity Press, 1984.

Gomez-Mejia, L., H. Tosi, and T. Hinkin. "Managerial Control, Performance and Executive Compensation." *Academy of Management Journal* 30, no. 3 (1987): 51–70.

Harbison, F., and C.A. Myers. *Management in the Industrial World.* New York: McGraw Hill, 1959.

Hashimoto, Masanori, and John Raisian. "Employment Tenure and Earnings Profiles in Japan and the United States." *American Economic Review* (September 1985): 721–35.

Hirschey, M., and J.L. Pappas. "Regulatory and Life Cycle Influences on Managerial Incentives." *Southern Economic Journal* 48, no. 10 (1981): 327–332.

Hofstede, Geert. *Cultures and Organizations: Software of the Mind.* London, McGraw Hill Book Company, 1991.

———. "Dimensions of National Cultures in Fifty Countries and Three Regions." In *Explications in Cross-Cultural Psychology* edited by J.B. Deregowski, S. Dziurawiec, and R.C. Annis. Lisse, The Netherlands: Soviets and Zeilinger, 1983, pp. 335–55.

———. *Culture's Consequences: International Differences in Work Related Values.* Beverly Hills, Calif.: Sage Publications, 1980.

Hogan, T., and L. McPheters. "Executive Compensation: Performance Versus Personal Characteristics." *Southern Economic Journal* 46, no. 4 (1980): pp. 1060–68.

Janakiraman, S.N., R.A. Lambert, and D.F. Larcker. "An Empirical Evaluation of the Relative Performance Evaluation Hypothesis." *Journal of Accounting Research* 30 (Spring 1992): 53-69.

Jensen, M., and K.J. Murphy. "CEO Incentives: It's Not How Much You Pay But How." *Harvard Business Review* 90 (May/June 1990): 138–53.

———. "Performance Pay and Top-Management Incentives." *Journal of Political Economy* 98, no. 4 (1990): 225-64.

Kahn, L.M., and P.D. Sherer. "Contingent Pay and Managerial Performance." *Industrial and Labor Relations Review* 43, no. 2 (1990): 107S–20S.

Kelly, L., A. Whatley, and R. Worthley. "Assessing the Effects of Culture on Managerial Attitudes: A Three Culture Test." *Journal of International Business Studies* (Summer 1987): 17–31.

Kerr, J.L., and R.A. Bettis. "Boards of Directors, Top Management Compensation, and Shareholder Returns." *Academy of Management Journal* 30, no. 12 (1987): 645–64.

Lambert, R.A., and D.F. Larcker. "An Analysis of the Use of Accounting and Market Measures of Performance in Executive Compensation Contracts." *Journal of Accounting Research* 25 (Supplement, 1987): 85–129.

———. "Golden Parachutes, Executive Decision-making, and Shareholder Wealth." *Journal of Accounting and Economics* 7, no. 4 (1985): 179–203.

Leonard, J.S. "Executive Pay and Firm Performance." *Industrial and Labor Relations Review* 43, no. 2 (1990): 13S–29S.

Lewellen, W.G., and B. Huntsman. "Managerial Pay and Corporate Performance." *American Economic Review* 60, no. 9 (1970): 710–20.

Lewellen, W.G., C. Loderer, and K. Martin. "Executive Compensation and Executive Incentive Problems: An Empirical Analysis." *Journal of Accounting
and Economics* 9, no. 12 (1987): 287–310.

Lewellen, W.G., C. Loderer, and A. Rosenfield. "Merger Decisions and Executive
Stock Ownership in Acquiring Firms." *Journal of Accounting and Economics* 7, no. 4 (1985): 209–31.

McGuire, J., J. Chiu, and A. Elbing. "Executive Incomes, Sales and Profits." *American Economic Review* 52, no. 9 (1962): 753–61.

Masson, R.T. "Executive Motivations, Earnings and Consequent Equity Performance." *Journal of Political Economy* 79, nos. 11/12 (1971): 1278–92.

Murphy, K. "Incentives, Learning, and Compensation: A Theoretical and Empirical Investigation of Managerial Labor Contracts." *Rand Journal of Economics* 17 (Spring 1986): 59–76.

———. "Corporate Performance and Managerial Renumeration: An Empirical
Analysis." *Journal of Accounting and Economics* 7, no. 4 (1985): 11–42.

Neghandi, Anant. "Cross Cultural Studies: Too Many Conclusions." In *Modern
Organizational Theory*, edited by A. Neghandi. (Kent: Ohio, 1975).

Nelson, James, and John Reeder. "Labor Relations in China." *California Management Review* 27, no. 4 (1985): 13-32.

Riahi-Belkaoui, Ahmed, Claude Perochon, M.A. Mathews, Bruno Bernardi, and
Youssef A. El-Adly. "Report of the Cultural Studies and Accounting Re-
search Committee of the International Accounting Sections." *Advances in
International Accounting* 4 (1991): 175–98.

Ronen, Simcha, and Oded Shenkar. "Clustering Countries on Attitudinal Dimensions: A Review and Synthesis." *Academy of Management Review* 10
(1985): 435–54.

Sloan, R. "Accounting Earnings and Top Executive Compensation." *Journal of
Accounting and Economics* 16 (January/April/July 1993): 56–100.

Townsend, Anthony M., K. Dow Scott, and Stephen E. Marrkham. "An Examination of Country and Culture-Based Differences in Compensation
Practices." *Journal of International Business Studies* 21, no. 4 (1990): pp.
667–78.

Tung, Rosalie. "Patterns of Motivation in Chinese Industrial Enterprises." *Academy of Management Review* 6, no. 3 (1981).

White, Michael. *Payment Systems in Britain*. Aldershot, England: Gower, 1981.

Index

Accounting environment, cultural variations in, 9–11, 120
Accounting principles, 40, 43–49
Accounting Principles Board (APB): Opinion No. 20, 47; Opinion No. 28, 41
Accounting techniques, conservatism principle in, 47–48
Accounting theory, 40–49; accounting postulates in, 40–41; accounting principles in, 43–49; contingency, 119–20; theoretical concepts in, 42–43
Accounting values model, 11
Adhikari, A. and Tondkar, R. H., study of, 119, 120, 122–24
Attitudes and values, cross-cultural research on, 8

Big Eight accounting firms, domination of standard-setting process by, 89
Big Six accounting firms, in study of perception of accounting concepts, 54

Capture theories of regulation, 85–86
Cognitive style, cultural research on, 8, 11–14

Compensation practices, 133–50; in collectivist versus individualist societies, 145; international differences in, 144–45; in masculine versus feminine societies, 145; measures of, 146; and power distance in society, 144; and uncertainty avoidance in society, 144–45; of U.S. executives, 133–43
Conservation task performance, and cognitive functioning, 12–13
Conservatism principle of accounting, 47–48
Consistency principle of accounting, 46–47
Contingency theory of international accounting, 119–20
Cost principle of accounting, 43–44
Cultural cluster model, and compensation practices, 144
Cultural determinism thesis, 39, 120; in compensation practices, 133–50; in disclosure requirements of stock exchanges, 120–26; in perception of accounting concepts, 49–61; in professional self-regulation, 92–97
Cultural relativism model, 3–14; accounting environments in, 9–11;

cognitive functioning in, 11–14; micro-organizational behavior in, 8–9;
operationalization of culture in, 3–6;
organizational structure in, 6–7
Culture: anthropological approaches
to, 1–3; defined, 53, 120; and judg-
ment/decision process, 3, 49–54;
value-system classification of, 1

Disclosure, accounting: accounting environment variables in, 9–10; and
composite-disclosure index, 122–24;
cultural determinism in, 120–22; full
disclosure principle in, 47; and value
orientations, 10–11
Disclosure requirements: in individualist versus collectivist society, 121,
124; in masculine versus feminine
society, 121–22, 124; and power distance orientation of society, 121;
regulatory, 47; of stock exchanges,
120–26; and uncertainty avoidance
orientation of society, 122, 124

Entity postulate of accounting, 40–41
Entity theory of accounting, 42–43
Evaluation system, and individual-
collectivism relationship, 7
Executive compensation (U.S.), and
firm performance, 133–43

Field dependence concept, 8, 13
Financial Accounting Standards Board
(FASB), 88–89; disclosure requirements, 47
Financial statements: and consistency
principle, 46–47; and full disclosure
principle, 47; and investment decisions, 9–10
Fund theory of accounting, 43

Going-concern postulate, 41
Gray, S. J., accounting values model
of, 11

Hierarchies, and power distance dimension, 7

Hofstede, G., classification of cultural
dimensions, 5–6, 7, 11, 92, 144

INDSCAL model, 57–58, 60–61
Intelligence, and cultural system, 13–
14
Interest-group theories of regulation,
85–86
International accounting: contingency
theory of, 119–20; emic versus etic
approach in, 60
Investment methods, European versus
U.S., 9–10

Job satisfaction, cultural research on,
8–9
Judgment/decision process, 3; cognitive
view in, 49–53; cultural view in, 53–
54; decision process in, 52

Market use agency, 86
Matching principle of accounting, 45–
46
Measurement of revenue, 44–45
Measurement procedure, and objectiv-
ity principle, 46
Metcalf Report, 89
Micro-organizational behavior, cross-
cultural research on, 8–9
Monitoring system, and uncertainty
avoidance, 7

Object representation, and cognitive
functioning, 12
Objectivity principle of accounting, 46
Organizational structure, effect of culture on, 5, 6–7

Perception of accounting concepts: and
judgment/decision process, 49–53;
study of, 54–61
Political ruling-elite theory of regulation, 86
Power distance, and professional self-
regulation, 92–93
Professional self-regulation, 92–97; in
individualist versus collectivist society, 93; in masculine versus feminine
society, 93; and power distance of

society, 92–93; and uncertainty avoidance of society, 93
Proprietary theory of accounting, 42
Psychological differentiation theory, 8
Public-interest theories of regulation, 85

Regulation: corporate costs of compliance, 91; debate on, 86; free-market approach to, 86–88; private-sector approach to, 88–89; public-sector approach to, 90–92; self-, cultural determinism in, 92–97; theories of, 85–86; in the United States, 47, 88–92
Revenue principle of accounting, 44–45
Revenues and expenses, and matching principle, 45–46
Reward system, and social division of sex roles, 7

Securities Acts of 1933 and 1934, 89, 90
Securities and Exchange Commission (SEC), 47; role of, 90–91; relationship with the FASB, 89

Self-regulation, cultural determinism in, 92–97
Spatial reference systems, cultural differences in, 13
Standards. See Regulation
Stock exchange disclosure requirements, 120–26; and composite disclosure index, 122–24; convergence hypothesis in, 126; and cultural dimensions of society, 120–22
Systems approach to culture, 1, 2

Theoretical concepts of accounting, 40, 42–43
TORSCA scaling routine, 55, 56–57

Unit-of-measure postulate, 41

Value systems approach to culture, 1, 2, 8
Values, accounting, 10–11

Work motivation, cultural research on, 8

Zones of accounting influence, 120

About the Author

AHMED RIAHI-BELKAOUI is Professor of Accounting in the College of Business Administration, University of Illinois at Chicago. A prolific author of journal articles and scholarly and professional books and textbooks, he serves on the editorial boards of numerous prestigious journals in his field and is known for his unusual, often groundbreaking research and analysis. This is his twenty-sixth Quorum book.

ISBN 0-89930-953-4

HARDCOVER BAR CODE